Contents

Introduction: How to Use This Book

One student ponders a challenging mathematical problem; another wants to know what garter snakes eat; a third plans to re-create a courtyard scene from a medieval castle; and a fourth student needs to find the best price for a full-suspension mountain bike. What do these students have in common? They each need to find the right information.

Why teach information skills? Because these are skills students will use their whole lives. Students who can systematically express and explore their ideas can experience satisfaction in learning. Their desire to know and understand increases with each deepening learning experience. As they find success on the steps of research, their confidence in their ability to gain and apply knowledge increases.

Information skills are called upon in every subject within the classroom walls, and in daily life beyond the walls. Students need these strategies to conduct primary and secondary research; to analyse, organize, and synthesize new information; to make connections with prior knowledge and experiences; and to gain new understanding of the processes and products of research. Their growing information skills can increase their independence as researchers and simultaneously help them develop collaborative skills.

This book of teaching plans provides comprehensive strategies for all three stages of information skills acquisition:

1. asking interesting questions worth exploring;
2. searching widely in various ways for possible answers;
3. making decisions based on discoveries, then sharing new understanding.

Use of the teaching plans is flexible. The plans can be easily adapted for grades 5 through 9. They can be used to guide students through a specific research project or to provide background skills. Although the lessons are logically grouped from the initial selection of a topic to the final publishing, it is not necessary to follow them in order. Related lessons are cross-referenced for your convenience. Adapt the order according to your preferences or needs. For example, you may wish to have students select a format early in a project, or at a later stage. Some classes might spend several lessons on developing library skills; others might skip the section entirely.

The teaching plans have several key features that will enhance their usefulness.

Information
Transformation

Teaching strategies for authentic research, projects, and activities

Tricia Armstrong

Pembroke Publishers Limited

Dedicated to Dan, Lisa, and Gaelen,
who know how to transform information into knowledge
and knowledge into wisdom

© **2000 Pembroke Publishers**
538 Hood Road
Markham, Ontario, Canada L3R 3K9
www.pembrokepublishers.com

Distributed in the U.S. by Stenhouse Publishers
477 Congress Street
Portland, ME 04101
www.stenhouse.com

We acknowledge the financial support of the Government of Canada through the
Book Publishing Industry Development Program (BPIDP) for our publishing
activities.

Canadian Cataloguing in Publication Data

Armstrong, Tricia, 1952-

Information transformation: teaching strategies for authentic research,
projects, and activities

Includes bibliographical references and index.
ISBN 1-55138-122-2

1. Research – Study and teaching (Elementary). 2. Information retrieval –
Study and teaching (Elementary). I. Title.

ZA3075.A75 2000   025.5'24'071   C00-931563-2

Editor: Kate Revington
Cover Design: John Zehethofer
Cover Photography: Ajay Photographics
Typesetting: JayTee Graphics

Printed and bound in Canada
9 8 7 6 5 4 3 2 1

Blackline Masters (BLMs)	Integral parts of many lessons
Strategy Spotlights	Summaries of useful strategies, ready to hand out
Do It Differently	Suggestions to accommodate multiple intelligences
Plug It In	Technology applications
Think It Over	Reflection and journalling prompts
Take It Further	Lesson extension ideas

Teaching Tips for Information Transformation

Here are some recommendations and insights to guide you in helping students develop their research skills.

PART A: THE RESEARCH PLAN

"First comes thought; then organization of that thought into ideas and plans; then transformation of those plans into reality. The beginning, as you will observe, is in your imagination."

— Napoleon Hill

- New knowledge inspires new questions. Be sure to generate adequate background knowledge before students embark on choosing topics. Whenever possible, let the students pick topics they are interested in or select their own narrow topics from a field you suggest. Students can post their choices and all classmates can contribute ideas about available resources and search strategies.
- Point out to students that the steps of selecting a topic, establishing a purpose, identifying the audience, and choosing a format can be challenging, even for professional writers. These four steps are interconnected and often change as the research progresses and the writer gets a clearer idea.
- Give as much importance to students' skills in asking questions as you do to their skills in answering them. Have class-wide discussions about students' questions on issues, events, and people; play question games; and institute a "Question of the Day" that students take turns contributing. Promote the value of questions that challenge thinking, encourage reflection, and draw on personal knowledge and experience.

PART B: THE SEARCH FOR INFORMATION

"I find that a great part of the information I have was acquired by looking up something and finding something else on the way."

— Franklin P. Adams

- Students can approach their searches with the thought that the information they want is out there somewhere. They simply need to adjust their search tools and strategies to find it. Share stories of your own experiences searching for information.
- Better search strategies yield better results. Encourage students to prepare before using technology. For example, they can select keywords before beginning an Internet search, and define needs and questions before phoning for information. Support students' use of technology to find, access, and organize information and data.

- Encourage students to make connections between their research discoveries and their own lives. Provide opportunities for them to analyse and reflect on texts to take information to a higher level of understanding.

PART C: THE TRANSFORMATION OF INFORMATION

"Technique is transitory. It helps us, but it is not the point. The point is what we do and why we do it."

— *Joseph Janes*

- Point out to students that skill in note taking and organizing is not so much a matter of what happens on the page: the process of identifying which information is important and how the pieces connect to the whole is what matters.
- Help students to become familiar with a wide range of organizational strategies, then let them choose what suits them best. Outlines are flexible. Encourage students to adjust their organization of information according to their preferences and the needs of the project.
- As they answer their inquiry questions, students can determine their point of view on the information collected and draw conclusions about their research. As students compare facts from different sources, challenge them to look for differences in similar ideas (analysis) and similarities in different ideas (synthesis).
- Provide many authentic, supportive experiences for sharing, teaching, and publishing information.
- Your involvement in teaching information skills structures independent learners. Your enthusiasm for information skills structures lively, inquisitive learners. Enjoy the process as well as the products!

Part A:

The Research Plan

Chapter 1

Get Ready for Research

Choose a Topic

STARTING POINTS

Objective: to establish personal relevance of topic

Skills at Work: celebrating, collaborating, deciding, generating

Activity: group discussion

Write this statement on the board: "No matter what you write about, you write about yourself." Ask students to consider whether they agree with the statement, then form into two groups based on their viewpoints. Members of each group can discuss their viewpoints, backing up their opinions with personal experiences of writing, reading, and viewing a variety of texts. Remind students to give everyone in the group a chance to express ideas. The group can make a summary of their ideas, then appoint one member to report to the class.

You might provide students with BLM: Start from What You Know Best (p. 38), to establish a list of starting points for writing topics.

Think It Over: Invite students to use a journal entry to explore this question: Why should I choose a topic I care about?

"WRITE" BEGINNINGS

Objective: to identify starting points for writing

Skills at Work: celebrating, evaluating, generating, identifying

Activity: discussion, writing

Ask students if they have ever had the experience of not knowing what to write about. What did they do? How did they come up with an idea?

Discuss these points with students: A basic rule of writing effectively is to write about yourself, the things you know and care about, and your experiences. Everyone's life is full of starting points for writing. Finding starting points is simply a matter of asking, "Who am I?" "What have I done?" "What do I care about?" If students need some help coming up with ideas, have them complete BLM: What Matters to You? (p. 39). Then they can write paragraphs expanding on two or three of their answers. The lists and paragraphs can be kept in their writing folders for later development.

Plug It In: Develop a list of Web sites for students to visit in their spare time that might spur their interest in new directions: museum and art gallery sites, science and nature sites, sites pertaining to various countries and local heroes, and so on. Perhaps the school librarian could help you. Encourage students to visit the sites and download images or text to create an electronic scrapbook of topics they would like to learn more about.

Objective: to expand starting points

Skills at Work: analysing, generating, summarizing, synthesizing

Activity: stream of consciousness writing

The following activity can be used as a warm-up to working on a writing project. Have students choose a starting point or idea they think they would like to write about. They could refer to their lists on blackline masters Start from What You Know Best or What Matters to You? Time them for five to ten minutes while they write everything they can about their idea, as fast as they can. Encourage them to write whatever comes to mind in point form, without worrying about spelling, punctuation, or grammar. Tell them to keep writing without crossing out or changing words. After the time has elapsed, they can read what they have written, and circle ideas that could be developed further. These ideas could be rewritten as questions they would like to answer.

You might want to distribute and discuss Strategy Spotlight: Generating Ideas, page 30. Students can refer to it and select ideas to try.

You may wish to have students complete BLM: Picture This (p. 40) to visually represent their ideas about the thought process. Their drawings can be posted in the classroom, grouped according to quotation used. Students can circulate and discuss similarities and differences of representations and points of view.

Do It Differently: Invite students to think of something they feel strongly about, then respond to these questions: What ideas come to mind when you think about this subject? Why do you feel strongly about it? What would you like to learn about it? Students can make sketches or mind maps to show their ideas. For more information on mind maps and other graphic organizers, consult Strategy Spotlight: Graphic Organizers, page 35, or Strategy Spotlight: Spin an Ideas Web, page 32.

NARROWING A TOPIC

Objective: to focus a topic

Skills at Work: classifying, deciding, identifying, synthesizing

Activity: exploring analogy, making flow charts, BLM: Narrow a Topic (p. 41)

Ask students to share their ideas about the meaning of this analogy: Choosing a topic is like deciding what to wear. (You consider the whole range of possibilities and narrow them down to make your choice.) Draw a flow chart on the blackboard to describe the process of selecting clothes. (What to wear? — a sweater — long or short sleeves? — long — pullover or cardigan? — pullover — blue or brown? — blue) Then suggest a broad topic, such as sports, animals, or a topic under study in a school subject. Ask for ideas how to narrow it down step by step. Record suggestions on the board in flowchart form.

Provide students with BLM: Narrow a Topic, so that they can practise narrowing a topic. Strategy Spotlight: Ten Ways to Narrow a Topic, page 31, can be distributed for students' reference. Ask for feedback in a few days or weeks to see which points they have tried and what success they have had.

Plug It In: Subject directories on the Internet are usually arranged hierarchically. Suggest that students trace and compare the paths of several subject directories to narrow a topic. The results of narrowing "sports" to "downhill racing" might be something like this:

www.dmoz.org (4 steps)
sports — bicycling — mountain biking — downhill
www.yahoo.com (5 steps)
recreation & sports — sports — cycling — mountain biking — downhill
www.looksmart.com (7steps)
lifestyle — sports — sports A-Z — sports C — cycling — mountain biking — races

Take It Further: After students consider how choosing a topic is like deciding what to wear, ask them what else the process can be compared to. Let students work with partners to create a simile for the process of choosing a topic (shopping for clothes, ordering food in a restaurant, deciding what to cook for dinner). They can explain pictorially or in paragraph form how the simile conveys meaning.

TOPIC AND FORMAT MATCHING

Objective: *to focus and expand topics*

Skills at Work: *classifying, deciding, evaluating, speculating*

Activity: *small group work, chart making*

Students can work in small groups to brainstorm topics that would be **unsuitable** for each of these formats: paragraph, research report, half-hour video, cartoon. (*Note: Include the format of an upcoming assignment.*) Each group can create a chart to record their responses. They can choose three different topics for each format and explain why they would be unsuitable (too broad, too narrow, not enough information available, doesn't suit format, and so on). Then they can choose three topics that are related to the unsuitable topics but that would work for the formats provided. For example, "The History of the World" is too broad for a paragraph topic, but could be a topic for a book, and "The Color of My Room" is probably too narrow for a research report, but could be a topic for a paragraph. Groups can compare results with one another and assess responses.

BECOMING AWARE OF PURPOSE

Objective: *to identify purposes*

Skills at Work: *analysing, classifying, generating, identifying*

Activity: *discussion, group work*

Establish the Purpose

Discuss with students recent trips they have taken. Ask where and why they travelled. Record their responses on the board in two columns: one for destination, the other for purpose. Then ask students to consider the various purposes listed. Group the responses into categories, such as pleasure, business, and education. What other reasons for travel can students identify? Add these to the list.

Then discuss what purposes people might have for writing. Some are similar to those for travelling: business, pleasure, entertainment. Students might also mention that people write to explain how something works, to show how to do something, to offer and defend an opinion, to show how things are similar or different, or to describe something. Students can work in partners or small groups to identify the purpose for recent reading, viewing, and writing they have done.

Plug It In: Prepare a list of sites for students to visit to determine purpose. Some sites could have more than one purpose (e.g., a site might be entertaining and informative), but students can determine which is the primary purpose. Students can work with partners or in small groups to find two examples for each category (to express, to inform, to persuade, and to entertain).

IDENTIFYING PURPOSE

Objective: to determine author's purpose

Skills at Work: analysing, deciding, evaluating, identifying

Activity: partner work, chart making

Collect, or have students bring in, a variety of short newspaper and magazine articles. Include some pieces that express opinions or seek to persuade (such as op ed or columns), that entertain (such as humor columns), that describe (such as travel columns), that inform (such as news, how-to's), and that express the self (such as poetry, short stories, columns). Ask students to work with partners to consider the author's purpose for each and sort the pieces into categories based on the purpose. They can compare their choices with those of other pairs and explain their reasons.

Provide students with a topic, such as music or sports. Invite them to determine a purpose, then write a paragraph. They can exchange paragraphs and guess each other's purpose.

Do It a Different Way: Ask students to find examples of writing that have more than one purpose. They can share their examples with a partner and see whether they identify the same purposes.

Plug It In: Direct students to locate Web sites that publish students' writing and determine the purposes of selections. One starting point is **www.cln.org/themes/publish**. They can also review book report sites and analyse reports for their purposes. If they have read any of the same books, they can compare opinions. Students might wish to write and submit book reports of their own, written to persuade, to inform, to express, or to entertain.

CHARACTERISTICS OF VARIOUS PURPOSES

Objective: *to identify purpose of text*

Skills at Work: *collaborating, evaluating, identifying, integrating*

Activity: *jigsaw group strategy, BLM: Understanding Purpose (p. 42)*

Divide the class into groups of four or five to create "home" groups. Then have students count off from 1 to 4. These numbers will determine their "working" groups. Ask the 1s to meet together, the 2s, and so on and assign each of the four working groups a purpose: to express, to inform, to persuade, or to entertain. Ask each working group to discuss how to recognize the characteristics of their purpose for oral, written, and visual texts, then fill out their section of BLM: Understanding Purpose. After that, direct the groups to find examples of various formats with the same purpose, and list them on the blackline master. They could focus on the classroom.

Next, ask students to reassemble in their home groups. Each person reports from the working group. Home group students can complete the remaining blackline master sections based on the reports.

Take It Further: Direct students to look over the writing in their writing folders and identify the purpose of each piece. They can analyse how the tone or mood of the pieces varies according to the purpose, and write and submit their analysis in paragraph form.

EFFECTS OF PURPOSE ON RESOURCE

Objective: *to determine other purposes*

Skills at Work: *analysing, deciding, evaluating, generating*

Activity: *brainstorming in small groups*

Ask students to work in small groups to choose a nonfiction text and brainstorm ideas of how the same topic could be used for a different purpose. For example, a book about the animals of Australia could suggest a humorous story about two animals comparing jumping ability (to entertain); a persuasive book about protecting the environment in which the animals live (to persuade); and a poem about the variety of animal shapes and sizes (to express). Students can present their ideas graphically using a storyboard or chart. A storyboard divides a story or visual presentation into key moments to help with planning. The story is broken into "cells" much like a comic strip, but instead of each cell providing direct speech, it provides a description of what the audience will see and hear.

Plug It In: Let students work with partners to select a Web site, identify its purpose, then brainstorm ideas for possible sites that could link to it. These sites can be imaginary. For example, for a skateboarding site students might suggest that a site showing skateboard tricks (to inform) could link to one featuring copies of letters boarders have written trying to get a skatepark built (to persuade); to a site of skateboard comics (to entertain); and to a site of personal highlights of boarding (to express). Advanced students could suggest actual sites that could connect (but are not presently connected).

Take It Further: Challenge students to consider how a book from one subject could be adapted for use in another school subject. For example, a book on problem solving in math could be rewritten to reflect geographical situations. You might ask groups to submit one page of suggested text for each of the four purposes that a particular book is adapted to.

Identify the Audience

MEDIA ANALYSIS

Objective: *to identify audience for multimedia resources*

Skills at Work: *analysing, evaluating, identifying, predicting*

Activity: *group work, BLM: Who's Out There? (p. 43)*

Borrow a variety of magazines from the library or ask students to bring in examples from home. Have groups of students browse through the magazines and decide the audience that each is aimed at. How did they decide? Content? Advertisements? Style? Something else? How specifically can they describe the audience?

Suggest to students that identifying the audience can also be applied to music, art, TV shows, movies, Internet sites, and other formats. Consider using BLM: Who's Out There? for an assignment in which students choose several formats, identify the targeted audience, and provide specific examples to explain their choices.

RESOURCE ADAPTATION

Objective: *to identify potential audiences*

Skills at Work: *deciding, identifying, predicting, summarizing*

Activity: *group work, book design*

Display a resource that all the students are familiar with, such as a textbook or CD-ROM, and ask: Who is the audience? How could this resource be used for another audience? What would have to be changed?

Next, have groups of students select a book, analyse who the intended audience is, select a new audience, and decide what and how changes need to be made. You may wish to have on hand some audience descriptions and pass them out at random to the students (grandparents in their eighties living in small towns; fourteen-year-olds who live on ranches or who love horses; business executives who own their own companies, and so on). Students should recommend changes to appearance, as well as contents, of resources. Each group can create a new jacket cover for their book, including a brief summary designed to appeal to the new audience. Have them summarize their ideas about changes to content on a graphic organizer and present their ideas to the class. Examples of graphic organizers can be found in Strategy Spotlight: Spin an Ideas Web, page 32, or Strategy Spotlight: Graphic Organizers, page 35.

Do It Differently: Let students experiment with writing poems for different audiences, such as peers, younger children, and adults. Supply students with the first line of a poem and have them write several versions. You might display the finished poems where students can circulate and read them, comparing similarities and differences, and identifying the audience for each.

Plug It In: Invite students to select a Web site and identify the targeted audience. They can record how the site would need to be changed to suit another audience. Remind students to be sure to note appearance changes as well as contents.

Take It Further: How will a change in audience affect how a resource is promoted or advertised? Direct students to create a plan for a new advertising and marketing scheme.

AUDIENCE APPEAL

Objective: *to choose language appropriate for audience*

Skills at Work: *deciding, integrating, predicting, synthesizing*

Activity: *letter writing*

Choose an issue currently being discussed in your community, such as an environmental concern, a change to school regulations, or an amendment to a bylaw. Ask students to choose two different audiences they could write to about the issue. The audiences should be very different, such as a cousin in another city and the mayor of the town, or an expert on the subject and a Grade 3 class. Remind students to state their views using appropriate language and style for each audience. After the first draft is complete, ask students to consider which letter was easier to write. Which was more difficult? Why? Allow students to exchange letters and offer feedback about whether the language and style were appropriate for the intended audience.

You may wish to combine this lesson with one dealing with formal, informal, and non-standard English. Formal language, suitable for formal letters and research reports, includes precise and often elevated vocabulary. Informal language, suitable for personal letters and conversations, is characterized by simpler sentences and contractions. Non-standard language, suitable for characterizations and small talk, is marked by slang and a limited vocabulary range. See if students can identify expressions that might belong to each of the categories. Can they suggest other uses for each language level?

Think It Over: Invite students to explore their own ideas about audiences in a journal entry. Which audiences are the easiest to write for? Why? Which are the most difficult to write for? Why? Who would be the ideal audience? Why?

Take It Further: Encourage students to rework their letters to become letters to the editor of a local newspaper. Have them take special care proofreading for grammar, spelling, and punctuation before submission. They might wish to use a computer to select an appropriate font, size, and style of print.

AUDIENCE AWARENESS

Objective: *to increase awareness of audience*

Skills at Work: *identifying, speculating, summarizing*

Activity: *brainstorming/writing in small groups*

Ask students to form into small groups and brainstorm answers to this question: "Why is it important to think about the audience when you write/create something?" Each group should create a one-paragraph answer to share with the class. As each group gives its answer, note the main points on the board. Then have the class note the similarities and differences of the answers. What conclusions can they draw? Which characteristics of the audience need to be considered? (age, background knowledge, opinion, education, and so on).

You might find it appropriate for students to complete BLM: Who Is My Audience? (p. 44) about a project they are working on now.

Take It Further: Students can form into two teams based on their reaction to this question: Is it important for an artist to think of the audience when creating? Each group should decide how to support their opinion, then create a one-paragraph answer to share with the class. Alternatively, the two teams could hold a debate.

Start Thinking About Formats

NONFICTION FORMATS

Objective: *to identify nonfiction formats*

Skills at Work: *identifying, generating, observing, predicting*

Activity: *categorizing, program conception*

Ask students to define nonfiction. Then create a three-column chart on the board with Listening/Speaking, Reading/Writing, and Viewing/Representing as the headings. Ask students to suggest nonfiction formats they have experienced for each of the categories. Some examples might overlap. Remind students to consider electronic, oral, and visual formats, as well as print media.

Have groups of students imagine they could create a specialty TV channel featuring nonfiction programs. Ask them to identify the theme of their station and five or six programs they would develop. For each program they can indicate the purpose and audiences and provide a one-paragraph synopsis of the content.

Take It Further: Suggest that students visit a library or bookstore to investigate categories of nonfiction. They could predict the ratio of nonfiction to fiction books, then check their predictions by counting the number of shelves of each at their visit.

EFFECTIVE FORMATS

Objective: *to identify formats*

Skills at Work: *classifying, deciding, generating, identifying*

Activity: *brainstorming, group work, checklist completion*

As a warm-up, have the class brainstorm a variety of oral, written, and visual formats, or forms. Record ten or twelve on the board. Then ask the class to form into an even number of groups (four or six) of about the same size. Tell each group to generate a list of ten famous people from a variety of fields (such as entertainment, sports, history, and politics). Then groups can exchange lists and students can decide which format(s) each person on their new list has used to share their knowledge or talents. For example, Martin Luther King, Jr., gave inspiring speeches, Jim Carrey acts and does comedy routines, and Georgia O'Keeffe painted. If time permits, repeat the activity, with each group first generating a list of formats, then exchanging lists and brainstorming names of famous people who use those formats.

To remind students of the wide range of formats, ask them to complete BLM: Fifty Formats Checklist (p. 45), to determine which common formats they have worked with. How to Show What You Know is a more complete listing of formats and appears as Appendix 1.

VARIOUS FORMATS, ONE PURPOSE

Objective: *to select appropriate formats*

Skills at Work: *collaborating, deciding, integrating, problem solving*

Activity: *group work, proposal making*

Ask students to form groups and choose an upcoming event, such as a school or community concert, sporting event, or performance. Then each group can decide how they would publicize the event. They can detail a proposal about the formats and the content they would include, showing how each would be used and developed. Remind students to consider various types of formats, including electronic and multimedia (or refer them to BLM: Fifty Formats Checklist or Appendix 1, How Can You Show What You Know?).

Take It Further: Students may be able to present their ideas directly to the people in charge of the event. Otherwise, illustrated proposals could be posted in the classroom.

FORMAT AFFINITY

Objective: *to identify personal preferences*

Skills at Work: *deciding, evaluating, identifying, problem solving*

Activity: *questionnaire, group discussion*

Discuss with students what formats they like to use best. Would they rather give a speech or write a letter? Why? Would they rather perform a pantomime or write a journal entry? Why? Emphasize that some students are naturally drawn to some formats and others to other formats. Ask why might this be so (personality, skill, experience). Bring out the point that ideally everyone can work in a role that is comfortable for them, but also can experiment with taking on different roles and responsibilities.

BLM: Personal Preferences (p. 46) raises questions students can respond to. Ask students who answer mostly "a" to meet together, mostly "b" to meet together, and mostly "c" to meet together. (If students had the same number for two letters they can make a choice.) Each group can look over their choices for that letter and discuss common characteristics. They can develop a list of tips for using those formats and become a panel of experts. Their names and list of tips can be posted in the classroom for other students to consult as they work with these formats.

If time allows, students might also group in their least favorite letter and discuss the situations under which they might be willing to give those formats a try.

FAVORITE FORMATS

Objective: *to classify formats*

Skills at Work: *analysing, classifying, identifying, predicting*

Activity: *group discussion based on BLM: Format Match-up (p. 47)*

This lesson is a variation on the previous lesson, "Format Affinity." Which formats would students recommend for someone who likes talking? (speech, oral report, audiotape). What about someone who likes writing? performing? Have students work in groups to complete BLM: Format Match-up. They can refer to BLM: Fifty Formats or Appendix 1 if they need a list of formats. Students can then meet with others according to their favorite category, and create a list of tips for using those formats.

PROJECT PLAN

Objective: *to select workable format for topic*

Skills at Work: *analysing, deciding, identifying, planning*

Activity: *completion of BLM: My Project (p. 48)*

If students are working on a project in a subject area, they can complete BLM: My Project to summarize ideas for their project. Depending on the project, students may prefer to select a format at a later stage, such as after research is complete.

Student Self-Assessment

Have students identify their strengths in these four areas: choosing a topic, establishing a purpose, identifying an audience, and selecting a format. Which aspects are the easiest? Which are the most challenging? Ask students to formulate goals for improving their skills. The goals can be referred to and refined throughout the school year.

Chapter 2

Ask Questions

Explore Personal Knowledge

WAYS TO AWAKEN PRIOR KNOWLEDGE

Objective: *to identify previous knowledge*

Skills at Work: *generating, identifying, summarizing*

Activity: *partner work, brainstorming, webbing*

This activity can be used as a warm-up to a new topic being introduced in class, or as a way to determine depth and breadth of personal knowledge on a subject.

Begin by asking students to consider what they know about the selected topic. They can each compress everything they know into two minutes, tell it to a partner, and then switch roles. Discuss with students: Telling someone is one way to find out what you know. How else might you do it? Ask students to brainstorm ways they could quickly outline, list, or organize their knowledge on a topic. If students are unfamiliar with webs (clusters), introduce their uses and let them work with Strategy Spotlight: Spin an Ideas Web, page 32. If students are familiar, you might distribute Strategy Spotlight: Here's What I Know, page 33. Prompt them to select a point they haven't tried before and to use that to brainstorm their knowledge.

If students are not currently working with topics, choose a topic related to one of their school subjects or a timely community event, and provide them with pictures, photographs, or artifacts relating to it. Have them follow the same steps of generating their prior knowledge, using the items as prompts.

Do It Differently: Have students identify their prior knowledge, then use the information to write a story or poem, or to create a flow chart or labelled illustration about the topic.

QUESTIONS TO LAUNCH RESEARCH

Objective: *to generate questions*

Skills at Work: *analysing, generating, identifying*

Activity: *Completion of BLM: I Know, I Wonder (p. 49)*

Once students have had a chance to explore their personal knowledge on a topic, they can formulate questions they would like to answer. Be sure to generate adequate background knowledge on a topic, such as by watching a video, reading an introductory book, or looking at pictures about the topic. The students can list their previous knowledge under "What I Know" on BLM: I Know, I Wonder. For each point, they can identify questions they would like to answer and write them next to the point, under "What I Wonder." Finally, they can consider the questions they've generated and answer the final question, "What do I want to find out about my topic?"

Make Personal Inquiries

5WH

Objective: *to formulate questions*

Skills at Work: *analysing, classifying, generating, speculating*

Activity: *brainstorming, question creation, BLM: 5WH (p. 50)*

Begin with a class brainstorm in which students raise questions about a topic under consideration in one of their school subjects. Have them orally contribute as many questions as possible in a minute or two, then have them consider which words began their questions. List the words on the board (what, where, who, and so on). Next, share the Kipling poem (from BLM: 5WH), either by reading it aloud or by writing it on the board.

Ask students what the poet means by "they taught me all I knew." These six ways of posing questions (Who, What, Where, When, Why, and How) are collectively known as 5WH. You might encourage students to take a few minutes to memorize the poem. Have them examine newspaper and magazine articles, highlighting information that answers Who, What, When, Where, Why, and How questions. For each case, they can invent the question that might have been asked. They can note and compare their findings, and consider where in the article the answers are found. Ask: Which type of questions are generally answered towards the beginning of the article? Why might that be?

Students might use BLM: 5WH to identify questions pertaining to research projects they are undertaking.

Do It Differently: Ask students to create a poem or visual representation of 5WH questions.

Plug It In: Bookmark, or list, interesting Web sites for students to visit. They can create a list of 5WH questions about the information at each site. If time permits, they can visit linked sites to see if any of their question are answered there.

Take It Further: Invite students to research biographical information about Rudyard Kipling and speculate how he might have come to the conclusion that his six "serving men" taught him all he knew. Let them discover what sorts of things Kipling wrote and how questioning might have helped him in his work.

SIGNIFICANT QUESTIONS

Objective: *to formulate questions*

Skills at Work: *generating, identifying*

Activity: *peer interviews*

Ask students to think of a hero, celebrity, or public figure and determine what one question they wish they could ask that person about his or her life. Once students have generated questions, they can share them and consider each others' responses. Is there anything they'd like to change about their questions, based on other responses? Next, ask students to choose three questions that they could use to bring out interesting and important information about someone's life. Students can then meet with partners and ask their three questions, taking note of the answers. Finally, each partner can create a brief biography based on the interview. The biography might be in the form of a short story, poem, or news report. Any print representation should include a cover page with artwork.

Take It Further: Tell students to formulate three questions about their research topics that they would like to be able to ask of a historic figure. They can exchange their questions with partners and write responses.

RESPONDING TO QUOTATIONS

Objective: *to apply prior experience*

Skills at Work: *deciding, generating, identifying, integrating, summarizing*

Activity: *class discussion, BLM: Question Quotations (p. 51)*

To encourage students to think actively about questions, write this stem on the board: A good question . . .

Ask students for suggestions about how they might finish the stem. Write some of their suggestions on the board and discuss. To expand upon students' ideas tell them to complete BLM: Question Quotations. You may wish to review the use of the anecdotal format (or whichever format you prefer the answers are in). Students could first do a rough draft, then exchange their writing with peers for feedback on organization, grammar, spelling, and punctuation.

Do It Differently: Some students might find it easier to represent the quotation visually. Give them the option of doing that and adding a caption that links the quotation with an experience they have had.

Make Group Inquiries

THE IMPORTANCE OF QUESTIONING

Objective: *to identify value of questions*

Skills at Work: *analysing, classifying, deciding, observing*

Activity: *class discussion, BLM: Classroom Questions (p. 52)*

You might begin by writing this saying on the board: "Ask a question and you'll be a fool for a minute. Don't ask, and you'll be a fool for a lifetime." Ask students to suggest what it means. Discuss the following questions with the class, encouraging students to draw on personal experiences: How do you feel about asking questions in class? Are there times when it's easier to ask questions? Are there times when you would like to know something, but don't ask? What keeps you from asking? Have you ever felt grateful that someone else has asked the question you were wondering about?

Direct students to form into small groups to answer the questions on BLM: Classroom Questions. Then each group can present its findings and you can organize and summarize the results of all groups on a chart. The class as a whole can draw conclusions about ways to increase interesting questions in the classroom.

If you have recently given an assignment, suggest students practise brainstorming questions now to identify what they need to know about the assignment. (When is it due? How shall I organize my work? Which resources should I use? How will I decide which information to include?)

Plug It In: Encourage students to compare data for the following Take It Further activity with other classes or schools via e-mail. How do the types and numbers of questions vary between schools via e-mail? How do the types and numbers of questions vary between schools, cities, or countries?

Think About It: Invite students to make a journal entry on a question they have wondered about for a long time. Ask them to consider how they have tried to answer or explore the question and what other ways they could try.

Take It Further: Ask students to predict the number of questions they raise on an average day. What kinds of questions do they ask? Who answers most of them? Have students keep track of all the questions they ask for one day, including both in and out of school times. They can tally their numbers, organize the questions in categories, and present the results to the class. The class can create a graph showing the average number and types of questions asked by students.

THE NATURE OF QUESTION GAMES

Objective: *to categorize question games*

Skills at Work: *classifying, collaborating, generating, identifying*

Activity: *group discussion*

Create a classroom display of games that are based on questions and answers. Ask students to share what they enjoy about each. Students could form into small groups and brainstorm games they know that rely on questions. Each group could consider one category, such as board games (Trivial Pursuit, Guess Who?), television and video games (Jeopardy), word games (Animal, Vegetable, or Mineral/21), and party games (Charades). After the groups have identified a number of games, they can establish common characteristics, sort them into sub-categories, and create a chart to compare and contrast the games. They can present their findings to the class. If time permits, students could play question games.

Take It Further: Invite students to generate ideas for new question-and-answer games. You could direct small groups to create a proposal for their game, identifying how it would be played and providing a few sample questions and answers. If time permits, they can develop their games, and exchange them with other groups to play.

**THE BENEFITS OF
BRAINSTORMING**

Objective: *to identify types of
questions*

Skills at Work: *classifying,
generating, identifying*

Activity: *group brainstorming*

Present students with a topic under discussion in one of their subjects or an extracurricular topic of interest to many students. Let them form small groups to brainstorm and record questions about the topic. Group members should contribute as many questions as possible in five minutes and record the questions in the order they were asked. Use of a tape recorder would make this easier, or else two members of the group could take turns recording the questions. Then to reinforce student experiences, distribute one copy of BLM: Questions, Questions, Questions (p. 53) to each group and have them respond to the questions about their experiences.

Take It Further: Connect question activities to other school subjects. In Math students can formulate questions and word problems for themselves and others to solve. In Social Studies and Science, students can formulate research questions and generate questions from direct observation. In English Language Arts students' questions can help deepen their understanding of texts and elements. Students can use questions in Fine Arts to learn more about how a piece of art was made and how it connects to their own creations.

**OPEN-ENDED QUESTIONS FOR
THE "EXPERTS"**

Objective: *to develop skill in
asking questions*

Skills at Work: *collaborating,
deciding, generating, problem
solving*

Activity: *group work*

Tell students to form into medium-sized teams based on a mutual interest or area of expertise. They can post their area of interest and invite questions on it, providing either a question box or sign-up list.

Each group can then work together to formulate three questions on each of the other groups' topics to add to the box/list. These questions should be asking for more than just surface knowledge or a yes/no answer. Once all the questions have been asked, groups can research and answer the questions. They can use a visual, written, or oral format, such as a pamphlet, panel discussion, or poster, to present their research.

Plug It In: Each group can collect its questions in a group folder. The results could be posted on a Web site which the group creates and designs specifically for the purpose. For related ideas on creating a Web site, see "Planning a Web Site Design" in Chapter 3, Create a Plan.

TEXT ANALYSIS

Objective: *to formulate levels of
questions*

Skills at Work: *comprehending,
generating, inquiring*

Activity: *group work on BLM:
Three Types of Questions
(p. 54)*

Distribute BLM: Three Types of Questions to students and read it over as a class. After explaining each type of question, ask students for examples of each, using a current topic of conversation in the classroom.

Then have students work in small groups to choose two questions of each type about a text all students are familiar with, such as the current chapter in Social Studies or Science. Each group member can record the questions on their copy of the blackline master. They can exchange their lists with another group's, answer the questions, then both groups can meet together to discuss the similarities and differences in the questions and answers.

Do It a Different Way: Have students analyse and compose questions about an audio or video production or about a painting, drawing, or sculpture (quite literally on the lines, between the lines and beyond the lines!).

Take It Further: Suggest that students devise test questions on material read. They can discuss various formats for test questions, such as multiple choice, true and false, short answer, matching, and so on. How are test questions different than research questions? Students could answer that question using a Venn diagram to compare and contrast.

QUESTION ASSESSMENT

Objective: to analyse Q & A formats

Skills at Work: analysing, classifying, deciding, evaluating

Activity: categorizing

An effective way to begin this lesson is to create a display (or ask students to bring in examples) of question-and-answer formats. You might feature Q and A books, printouts of FAQs, or Frequently Asked Questions, and columns from newspapers or magazines. Have students work in groups to analyse the questions. Which do they consider good questions and why? Which questions prompt new questions? Which ask for facts, which for opinions? How could the questions be improved? Students can investigate and report on various sources that answer questions (Web sites, books, columns, and so on), identifying the types of questions/answers, and speculating on how the answers are found.

PICTURE FOCUS

Objective: to generate questions

Skills at Work: analysing, deciding, generating, identifying, integrating

Activity: group brainstorming, observing

Post six or eight pictures around the classroom, each with a page beneath for recording questions. Choose the pictures, which could range from photographs to paintings/drawings, according to a high interest level — there should be a variety of things happening in each picture. If the students are currently researching topics, consider selecting pictures about those topics. Form students into groups of three or four, and ask each group to choose a picture to start with. Time students for two minutes at each picture, while they record as many questions as they can think of about the picture on the page provided. One member of the group should record the questions as they are asked. At the end of two minutes, each group moves on to the next picture and reads the questions already asked. Then they have two minutes to think of other questions about the topic. This exercise will become increasingly challenging as it proceeds. When all the groups have brainstormed all the pictures, discuss their experiences. What was easy about the activity? What was difficult? Did previous questions suggest new questions? You can assess groups according to the quality of questions asked.

Take It Further: Suggest that each group brainstorm questions about individual members' topics. Doing this will give students new directions to pursue in their research.

THE VALUE OF VENN DIAGRAMS

Objective: to compare and contrast a discussion and a brainstorm

Skills at Work: analysing, classifying, integrating, organizing, synthesizing

Activity: discussion, Venn diagram

Write this question on the board: What's the difference between a group discussion and a group brainstorm? Ask students to share their ideas, drawing on personal experience, and considering differing characteristic uses of each format. As students contribute ideas, organize the information into a Venn diagram with sections for Group Discussion, Group Brainstorm, and both. Alternatively, if the students are familiar with Venn diagrams, you might have them complete these activities with partners. When they are finished, pairs of partners can meet together to compare charts and add any additional points.

You may wish to extend this lesson by including either or both of the following lessons, "Group Roles in Research" and "Group Dynamics."

GROUP ROLES IN RESEARCH

Objective: to set personal goals

Skills at Work: analysing, deciding, identifying, predicting, problem solving

Activity: discussion and partner work

Ask students to consider this question: At what stages of the research process is a group helpful? Invite students to give specific examples with their suggestions, drawing on their previous experiences working in groups. Answers might include brainstorming, solving problems, giving and receiving feedback, making decisions, performing experiments, and doing Internet searches. Next, have students identify roles in group work. Record responses on the board.

You might want to have students work with partners to brainstorm skills needed for various group roles and chart their results. Partners can compare their lists with those of other groups, and make personal lists of strengths, skills they would like to improve, and steps they could take to improve them.

Take It Further: Students can choose what they consider the most important skill in group work ("respect other views," "give everyone a chance to speak") and create a banner advertising the skill to hang in the classroom.

GROUP DYNAMICS

Objective: to identify group dynamics

Skills at Work: evaluating, observing, speculating

Activity: discussion and observation of model group

There are many steps of the research process that can include input from a group, such as brainstorming questions, dividing research responsibilities, and making sense of information. Write this stem on the board and discuss students' suggestions for completing it: "It's easy to work in a group when . . . " Record some of the students' suggestions on the board. Then do the same for "It's difficult to work in a group when . . ." Ask students to contribute other ideas about the action each group member can take to help the group work effectively. Then call for about six volunteers to serve as a model group. Give the model group a task, such as coming up with an idea for a new video game. Members should decide on the basic components and objectives of the game, its name and the age group it will appeal to. Tell the students that they will be on display as they interact, and that they will have to stay focused as they will have only ten minutes to discuss their game and choose its name. They should try to include every group member, to listen attentively and build on one another's ideas, to encourage and support communication, and to stay on task as they work towards a consensus. The other class members can gather around the model group and take notes as the discussion proceeds, perhaps answering question 1 of BLM: Group Dynamics (p. 55). During the discussion, only the members of the model group should speak, although there can be an occasional reminder of the passing time. After the discussion is finished, ask the observers and participants for feedback on their observations of the discussion. Did the group achieve its goal? Did all members contribute, and were their ideas respected? What could the group improve in future discussions? Encourage students to make comments about the group as a whole, rather than about specific individuals. Provide all students with an opportunity to complete BLM: Group Dynamics.

Student Self-Assessment

Have students identify their strengths in these areas: asking questions, making personal inquiries, and making group inquiries. Which aspects are the easiest? Which are the most challenging? Ask students to formulate goals for improving their skills. The goals can be referred to and refined throughout the school year.

Chapter 3

Create a Plan

Understand the Nature of Research

RESEARCH IN A PERSONAL CONTEXT

Objective: to learn steps of research

Skills at Work: identifying, integrating, organizing, planning, problem solving

Activity: anecdote sharing, completion of BLM: Using Research Skills (p. 56)

Write the word "research" on the board and have students examine its roots (re-search: to search again). Ask them to consider when they have used research. Brainstorm for answers and record them on the board, using a web, an effective way of developing subtopics and details around main headings. Draw out experiences from daily life, such as shopping for a new bike or stereo and finding out what movies or TV shows are on. Find out how students got the information needed to make a choice. Discuss nonfiction authors the students are familiar with and explore how the authors got their information. Have students complete BLM: Using Research Skills. They can share their responses with one another and add any points they've overlooked. You may wish to have students complete the blackline master over several weeks' time as they observe their skills in action. Or, you may wish to have them complete the blackline master again in several months to check how their usage has grown.

Point out that effective research needs a plan. Invite students to talk about when they have made a plan to research, such as deciding to visit the local bike stores and compare prices, or deciding to check different search engines to find Web sites on magic tricks. Ask: Which planning strategies worked? Which didn't? Why not? What might students do differently next time?

You could also distribute Strategy Spotlight: See for Yourself, and Make Conclusions, page 34, as a model for scientific inquiry. If students are already familiar with the steps, have them adapt it for other types of research.

Take It Further: Encourage students to interview family members about when they have created and followed a plan, asking what they learned, what they'd do differently next time, and what advice they have about making a plan. Ask students to summarize their findings and report to the class.

Write these expressions on the board:

"Well begun is half done." (proverb)

"The beginning is the most important part of the work." (Plato, *The Republic*)

Ask students whether they agree with these statements and to support their opinions with examples from personal experiences. To reinforce the statements, ask students to represent one of the expressions in a visual format, such as on a poster, banner, sign, or bumper sticker. Advise students to carefully consider their choices for size, style, and type of font or lettering they will use, so that it will suit the format, the purpose, and the audience. You may find it effective to display the finished representations in the classroom, or students can post them at home near their work areas.

Think About It: Invite students to make a journal entry about their skills in creating and following a plan. What do they think is the importance of such skills? How do they predict using them beyond the classroom?

Apply a Plan

Make a list of group project formats that might be completed in your classroom, such as doing a research report, putting on a puppet play or reader's theatre production, making a newspaper, conducting an interview, or making a video. If there are other projects coming up in the classroom, such as science fair projects or a school function, use those. Divide the class into small groups and give each a format for which they will create a generic plan and draw up a list of steps that need to be followed. The steps should identify the variety of group roles that need to be undertaken. All of these plans could then be posted in the room, or bound as a reference for the class to use.

Explain to students that keywords can be used to search indexes, tables of contents, library catalogues, CD-ROMs, encyclopedias, and the Internet. Remind students that keywords can also be used to locate information on a page through skimming and scanning. Choose a topic, such as "What do wolves eat?" or "How is information stored on a CD-ROM?" Ask students to brainstorm possible keywords that could be used to search for the answer. Record their responses on the board and discuss possible refinements. Then ask students to consider keywords for their own research topics. They should be able to identify at least six keywords. In order to generate a good list, students can refer to notes on their topic and questions they have identified. BLM: Identifying Keywords can be used for listing their keywords.

Plug It In: For more activities using keywords electronically, see "Search Tools" in Chapter 4, Identify and Evaluate Sources, Materials, and Tools, and "Boolean Logic" in Chapter 5, Access Information.

LOOKING AT INFORMATION TECHNOLOGY

Objective: *to assess computer skills*

Skills at Work: *deciding, evaluating, identifying, planning*

Activities: *completing blackline masters Electronic Equipment Checklist, Computer Functions Checklist and Spreadsheet Functions Checklist (pp. 58, 59, 60)*

Before students go on to the stages of locating and accessing information, you may wish to have them assess their skills in using electronic equipment. They can identify the areas in which they would like to improve their skills and make plans for how they can do so.

Use BLM: Electronic Equipment Checklist to assess their familiarity with a variety of equipment, BLM: Computer Functions Checklist to assess their familiarity with basis computer functions, and BLM: Spreadsheet Functions Checklist to assess their familiarity with spreadsheet operations. If students are completing these checklists early in the school year, you may wish to have them fill in the blackline masters again near the end of the year to assess what they have learned. You may also want to add other equipment or functions to the lists based on what is available at your school.

Plug It In: Are students aware of what a virus check program is and how it works? What other technical problems do they know how to troubleshoot? Discuss situations appropriate to their skill levels, such as how to load software and how to determine hardware-software compatibility.

Take It Further: Invite students to research technological developments in order to develop an electronic timeline showing the evolution and use of various types of electronic equipment. Common types of equipment are listed on BLM: Electronic Equipment Checklist; terms are defined in the Glossary.

Organize a Plan

PLANNING A WEB SITE DESIGN

Objective: *to use organizers for planning*

Skills at Work: *classifying, identifying, integrating, organizing, planning*

Activity: *small group work*

Distribute Strategy Spotlight: Graphic Organizers, page 35. Discuss with students which organizers they have used and what they feel are the advantages and disadvantages of each. Advise students that although these are some commonly used organizers, students can adapt them to their own uses or create organizers of their own. Ask students to form small groups, select an organizer to collect, and plan ideas for designing a Web site. They can use their organizer to record the various steps of their plan. After they are finished planning, direct them to post and compare their organizers and discuss how using the organizer helped them create a plan.

Plug It In: Have groups of students work together to follow their plan for creating Web sites. Encourage them to first make a storyboard or other visual representation of the site and present it to you for approval. Building Web pages can involve Hypertext Mark-up Language (HTML) coding. If students are unfamiliar with HTML, they can locate a software program that allows them to build a site in an environment similar to word processing. Suggest that they start with a subject directory to find information on Web page development and graphics.

Set Goals

An effective way to present the process of creating a research plan is to distribute and review Strategy Spotlight: Developing a Research Plan, page 36. Depending on the type and length of project, students could design their own daily or weekly goal chart. Advise students that they may need to change their plan along the way depending on information they find or resources they wish to use. Establish what the procedure is for making a change. Do they need to clear changes with you or identify the change on their plan sheet?

Think About It: Have students explore these questions in a journal entry or class discussion: What goal would you like to achieve by following your plan? What skills would you like to improve?

Do It Differently: Encourage students to choose a format for their plan. They might turn it into the story of a quest or a recipe for combining sources, materials, and tools. It could become a storyboard or comic strip.

Plug It In: Let students use computer software to create their goals, checklists, and contracts.

Student Self-Assessment

Have students identify their strengths in creating plans and setting goals. How would they like to improve their skills? Students can formulate specific goals they would like to achieve and identify a time frame for reaching their goals.

Strategy Spotlight: Generating Ideas

Start a notebook that you can carry with you to jot down ideas as you get them. These ideas can become starting points for writing. Try any of the following suggestions to help generate ideas.

1. What's happening?

What's happening around you right now? Make a list of what you see, hear, smell, taste, and feel. Make lists in different places at different times. Imagine you are a detective and you are recording clues. Turn some of your clues into questions, such as "Who is the person in the phone booth talking to?" "Why does that dog keep following me?" and "How do they get the filling in the chocolate bar?"

2. Who said that?

Keep track of quotations that you like. Jot down quotations from friends and family, from TV shows and movies, and from newspapers and magazines. A librarian can help you find quotation collections in the library. A search on the Internet using "quotations" as a keyword will bring many results. Use a quotation as the centre of a mind web (which your teacher will explain) and explore other ideas it makes you think of. Connect it to your experience and to other texts you have read, seen, or heard.

3. What's in print?

Browse through resources, such as encyclopedias, CD-ROMs, Internet sites, dictionaries, and magazines. Jot down words that appeal to you, ideas that interest you, and facts that surprise you. Make a note of your reaction to information by adding big question marks or exclamation marks, happy faces, or other symbols.

4. Who likes what?

Ask friends and family about hobbies, skills, and experiences. Imagine you are a reporter interviewing them for a newspaper article. Find out what they like and why they like it. What information or experience have they had that has been important or surprising to them? Jot down any words, ideas, or information that interests you, and note how you feel about the information.

5. What if . . .

What if you had any ability or knowledge? What if you became your favorite character in a book, TV show, or movie? How would your life change? What would you accomplish if you lived in another time or environment? What information would you need to be successful? Jot down your impressions of the advantages and disadvantages of changing time or places.

Strategy Spotlight: Ten Ways to Narrow a Topic

If you have a general idea of a topic and need to narrow it down, try one or more of these techniques.

1. Choose a reference book or CD-ROM about the topic and look at the illustrations and photographs.

2. Check children's books for a general overview of the subject.

3. Open a resource book about the topic to any page. Write down three interesting things about the text or pictures on that page.

4. Open a resource book to five different pages. Write down one interesting fact or opinion from each page.

5. Check with your school librarian for suggestions.

6. Look at the subtopics listed in an encyclopedia index.

7. Survey people and ask, "When you think of _____, what comes to mind?"

8. Find your general topic in a library catalogue. Check for subtopics.

9. Watch a video about the topic.

10. Compare the categories of several Internet subject guides.

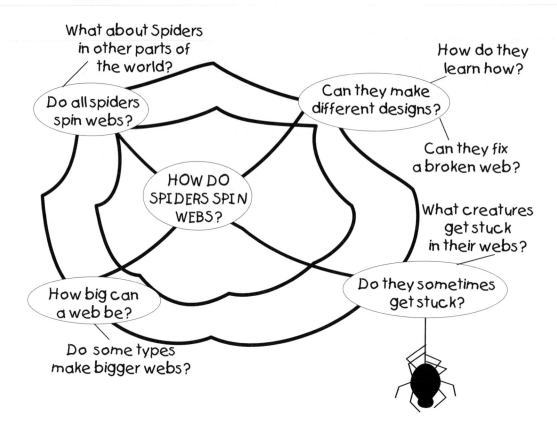

Webs are sometimes called cluster charts, mind maps, or spider maps. They can help you organize your ideas, information, and questions. Here is one way you can make a web:

1. Write your topic in the form of a question in the centre of a circle.

2. What do you want to know about your topic? Write each question you have in an attached circle. Add as many more circles as you need, remembering that they don't have to be in any special order. Don't worry about how good they look. Just add whatever you think of.

3. What ideas come to mind when you think of your questions? Write ideas, information, or other questions at the end of each ray. Add as many rays as you need. Use point form. Keep adding more ideas, information, and questions.

4. When you can't think of anything else to add, look back over your web. Highlight the ideas you like best.

Strategy Spotlight: Here's What I Know

How do you find out what you already know about a topic? Try any of these ideas. Don't judge your work at this stage. Just bring out your ideas in any order. Don't worry about spelling. Your focus is to get information onto the paper.

- Make a list. If you're handwriting, use point form. Skip a line between points in case you want to cut apart your list later to organize it. If you're using a computer, press **enter** after each point. You can use cut and paste later to organize your ideas.

- Time yourself and write non-stop for ten minutes about your topic. Don't judge the quality of what you write, and don't let your pencil (or fingers on the keyboard) stop moving. Keep writing. If you're stuck, write the name of your topic over and over until you get going again.

- Make a cluster or web of your knowledge.

- Make a tape recording of yourself telling everything you can think of about your topic.

- Tell a partner what you know. When you run out of ideas, prompt your partner to ask you questions to bring out more information.

- Look at pictures of your topic and write down information that comes to mind as you look at them.

- Write a table of contents for a book about your subject. Write down the headings you could use, then list what you know under each heading.

- Sketch what comes to mind when you think of your topic. Write point-form notes about each part of your sketch.

- Use your senses. Think of your topic and describe what you might hear, see, feel, taste, and smell in connection with it. Then take each of those ideas and jot down ideas expanding on them.

- Make a list of words about your topic. You could write at least one word for every letter of the alphabet. Or you could write as many words as you can think of for each of the letters in your topic's name.

- Make a timeline or flow chart.

- Compare your topic to another topic. Make a chart of the similarities and differences between the topics.

Strategy Spotlight: See for Yourself, and Make Conclusions

One way of conducting research is to find out for yourself: conduct an experiment, do field research, or make a survey.

The steps below are about planning an experiment to determine if the amount of water is the reason a plant is not growing well. They provide a model for conducting scientific research. As you read the steps, think about how you could use them for other types of research.

1. **Ask a cause-and-effect question.**
   A cause-and-effect question considers how the variables (things that can change) affect the result.
   "How does the amount of water affect the growth of my plant?"

2. **Restate the question in the form of a hypothesis.**
   A hypothesis is a guess of a possible answer to the cause-and-effect question.
   "More water will make my plant grow faster."

3. **Develop a procedure to test the hypothesis.**
   Which variable will you test? (amount of water)
   How will you measure it? (with a measuring cup)
   How will you control the other variables? (keep the plant in the same place, don't increase or decrease misting or fertilizer, use the same temperature of water, water at the same time of day)

4. **Identify and evaluate the necessary materials and tools.**
   What do you need? (measuring cup, thermometer, water)
   Are there safety considerations?
   How will you record your data? (make a chart of watering)

5. **Carry out the research.**

6. **Organize and record the data.**

7. **Analyse and interpret the data, looking for patterns and relationships.**

8. **Form conclusions based on the data, and compare them with the hypothesis. Evaluate the process and the conclusions.**
   Were there variables you overlooked?
   Does your hypothesis need to be revised?
   If you were to repeat the research, do you think you would get the same results? Would you do anything differently?

9. **Communicate the procedure and results of the experiment.**
   Share the results by summarizing the steps of your research.
   Consider using multimedia presentations and including visuals, such as charts, graphs, and illustrations.

How do you keep track of ideas and details? Try using a graphic organizer! You can use any of the graphic organizers shown here, or change them to suit your needs. You can even invent your own organizer! Some common uses are given, but each organizer can be adapted for other uses.

1. **Web**
   Discover how ideas connect.

2. **Flow Chart**
   Show steps or procedures.

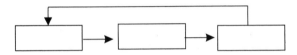

3. **Timeline**
   Display a sequence of events.

4. **Events**
   Decide how events connect.

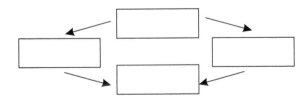

5. **Venn Diagram**
   Compare and contrast.

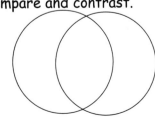

6. **Storyboard**
   Show scenes from a video or screens on a Web site.

7. **Two-Column Chart**
   Collect and organize information.

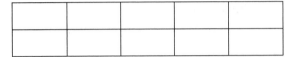

8. **Herringbone Chart**
   Divide one topic into many subtopics.

9. **Classification Chart**
   Sort facts into categories and compare data.

10. **Tree Diagrams**
    Break a large topic into several categories.

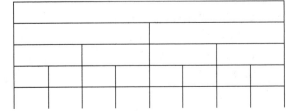

You can use these steps to guide your research plan.

1. **Choose a limited topic instead of a broad one.**
   Phrase your topic as a question. Establish a **purpose**, identify your **audience**, and select a **format**. You might make changes to these as you work, but it will help you get started if you make some initial decisions.

2. **Make a chart of what you know and what you wonder about your topic.**
   Use 5WH question to guide you (Who, What, Where, When, Why, and How). Write down five to ten questions.

3. **Create a plan.**
   Set goals for what you want to accomplish by a certain time. Identify keywords to guide your research.

4. **Identify sources of information about your topic.**
   Use point form and your own words to take notes. Record bibliographic information about the sources you use. Try to use several or all of these sources:
   a. **Direct observation:** Is there an experiment you can conduct to find answers? Is there a way for you to gather information through observation?
   b. **People:** Take notes as you talk to teachers, elders, experts, and classmates. Can they offer suggestions? Can they recommend books, videos, or Web sites?
   c. **Print:** Check classroom resources first, then use library resources. Search for books, magazines, and references, such as encyclopedias. Use the table of contents, index, and chapter headings to help you find information. Choose up-to-date references whenever possible.
   d. **Electronic:** Search electronic databases, Web sites, and CD-ROMs. Watch videos about your topic.

5. **Evaluate your sources.**
   How old is the information? Is the source an authority? Might the source be biased or presenting only one side of an issue?

6. **Make sense of information.**
   Reread information to understand why it might be important to your topic and how it connects with other information you know. Does it answer your questions? Is it important? interesting?

7. **Organize and record your information on an outline or graphic organizer.**

8. **Evaluate information.**
   Have you shown all sides of an issue? Are there any gaps in your information? Do you have visuals, such as photographs, graphs, and charts? Does the information suit your topic, purpose, audience, and format?

9. **Share what you know.**
   Ask for feedback from a classmate, then revise, edit, and proofread your work.

10. **Evaluate the process and the product you created.**
    What worked particularly well? What could you improve the next time?

Strategy Spotlight: Setting Goals

Clear goals will help you organize your research steps.

1. Decide on the goal you want to achieve and the date you want to achieve it by. Post your goal in a variety of places where you will see it.

2. Break your goal into parts or steps and decide the dates you want to achieve each step by.

3. What do you need to help you achieve each step? Who can help you? Which materials, tools, or resources do you need to gather? List them beside each step.

4. Make a checklist showing all of number 1, 2, and 3 above. Check off the steps as you complete them.

5. Make a contract promising yourself or your teacher that you will complete certain steps by certain dates. Specify that you will ask for help right away if you fall behind schedule.

Start from What You Know Best

What do you know best? Yourself, of course! Finish the following sentence stems about who you are, what you know and care about, and what you have experienced. Then use any of your answers as starting points for writing.

1. My favorite topics to read about are

2. Three things I like to do are

3. I would like to meet

   because

4. My dream vacation is

5. If I were in charge of my community I would make these three changes:

6. My favorite belonging is

   because

7. A sport I would like to try is

   because

8. A job I would like to have one day is

   because

9. One of the most important things I know is

10. My favorite memory is

What Matters to You?

If you want to write well, write about things you know and care about. List your answers to the categories below. Then choose any of your answers to develop as writing projects.

1. My favorite . . .
   (a) pastime
   (b) sport
   (c) animal
   (d) movie
   (e) book
   (f) subject

2. People who inspire me (friends, celebrities, historical figures)
   (a)
   (b)
   (c)
   (d)
   (e)
   (f)

3. Issues I really care about
   (a)
   (b)
   (c)

4. Places I care about
   (a)
   (b)
   (c)

5. Plans and ideas that inspire me
   (a)
   (b)
   (c)

6. Topics I would like to know more about
   (a)
   (b)
   (c)

Picture This

What's your idea about ideas? What does an idea look like? Read each of these quotations. Then choose one to illustrate on a separate piece of paper. Add the quotation as a caption for your picture.

"Ideas are like rabbits. You get a couple and learn how to handle them, and pretty soon you have a dozen."

— *John Steinbeck*

"The best way to get a good idea is to get a lot of ideas."

— *Linus Paley*

"The probability is that 999 of our ideas will come to nothing, but the thousandth one may be the one that will change the world."

— *Alfred North Whitehead*

"An open mind collects more riches than an open purse."

— *Will Henry*

Narrow a Topic

Practise narrowing a broad topic into a specific topic. Begin with the first box in each row and choose more specific topics as you cross the row. The topic in the last box of each row should be suitable for a one-page report. To sharpen your focus, phrase the topic as a question.

   Choose your own topic to narrow down in the last row. The first row is done for you.

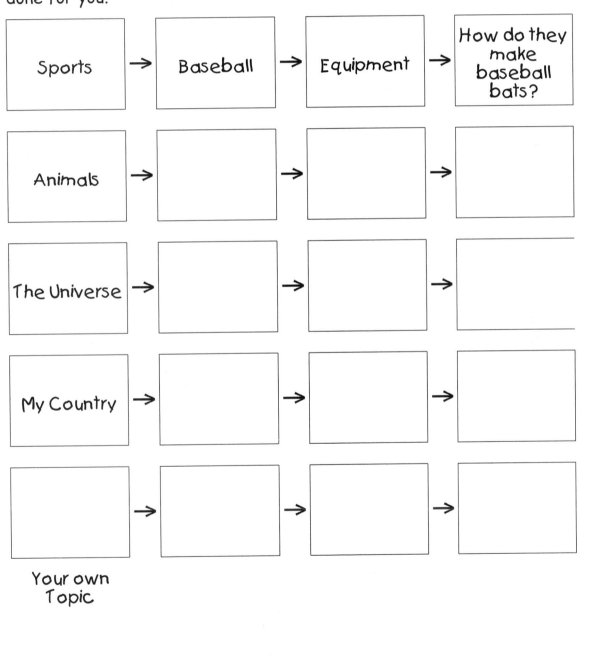

Sports → Baseball → Equipment → How do they make baseball bats?

Animals → → →

The Universe → → →

My Country → → →

Your own Topic → → →

Understanding Purpose

What are the clues that reveal a specific purpose? Meet in your working group and discuss your purpose. Decide together what characteristics it has and record them below. Then find examples in your classroom of formats with your purpose. List them below. Finally, meet in your home group and present your results. Complete the rest of the chart.

Purpose: to express

Characteristics

Examples

Purpose: to inform

Characteristics

Examples

Purpose: to persuade

Characteristics

Examples

Purpose: to entertain

Characteristics

Examples

Think About It

How does understanding the purpose help you to communicate more effectively?

Who's Out There?

Who is the audience?
List one example for each category. Explain who you think the ideal audience is and how you decided. Be specific in your description.

	Specific description of ideal audience	How I decided
TV show:		
Book:		
Magazine:		
Movie/Video:		

Think About It

Why is it important for an author to know who the ideal audience is?

Who Is My Audience?

Knowing who your audience is will help you to decide which information to include in a project and how to say it. Imagine your audience knows less about your topic than you do. What do you imagine the audience feels about your topic? Does the audience agree with your point of view?

Complete this page about a project you are working on now.

1. Draw a picture of your audience. (Use another page.)

2. My audience is similar to me in these ways:

3. My audience is different than me in these ways:

4. My audience knows the following about my topic:

5. My audience feels this way about my topic:

6. These are the questions my audience might ask me about my topic:

Think About It

How would you like your audience to feel about your topic?

Fifty Formats Checklist

There are many ways to share what you know. Which of these formats have you used? Put a check next to each one you've worked with. If a listing is unfamiliar, look it up in a dictionary. List any other formats you can think of at the bottom of the blackline master. After you have finished, look back over the whole list. Circle the formats that you would like to use sometime in the future.

__ advertisement	__ flow chart	__ poster
__ audiotape	__ game	__ puppet play
__ autobiography	__ glossary	__ questionnaire
__ biography	__ illustration	__ report
__ book	__ interview	__ review
__ book report	__ journal	__ role play
__ brochure	__ letter	__ script
__ cartoon	__ list	__ sign
__ comic strip	__ magazine article	__ slide show
__ commercial	__ mural	__ speech
__ dance	__ music	__ spreadsheet
__ database	__ newspaper article	__ storyboard
__ diary	__ oral report	__ survey
__ diorama	__ panel discussion	__ timeline
__ drama	__ paragraph	__ video
__ drawing	__ photo essay	__ Web page
__ essay	__ poem	

Other formats I can use:

Personal Preferences

Suppose you were given an assignment and had your choice of three different ways to represent it. Which would you choose? Select an answer for each of the following categories and circle it. More than one answer might appeal to you, but try to select the one you'd most likely choose.

1. Would your rather . . .
   (a) make up a song?
   (b) draw a picture?
   (c) make a sculpture?

2. Would you rather . . .
   (a) be the voice of a puppet in a puppet play?
   (b) direct a puppet play?
   (c) design the puppets for a puppet play?

3. Would you rather . . .
   (a) discuss a topic?
   (b) read about a topic?
   (c) build a model of a topic?

4. Would you rather . . .
   (a) sing a solo?
   (b) teach someone a song?
   (c) sing in a choir?

5. Would you rather . . .
   (a) work with a partner?
   (b) work by yourself?
   (c) work with a group?

6. Would you rather . . .
   (a) give a speech?
   (b) write a speech?
   (c) listen to a speech?

7. Would you rather . . .
   (a) hear instructions?
   (b) see a flow chart of instructions?
   (c) discuss instructions one step at a time?

8. Would you rather . . .
   (a) tell a story?
   (b) make a poster?
   (c) make a scrapbook?

Total number of "a" answers:
Total number of "b" answers:
Total number of "c" answers:

Think About It

What conclusions can you draw about the type of formats you prefer?

Format Match-up

Consider the qualities of people described below. What kinds of formats would each group likely prefer to use? Try to think of at least four formats for each group.

likes talking

likes thinking and imagining

likes building things

likes physical activities

likes art, music, and poetry

likes making charts and diagrams

likes working alone

likes working with others

My Project

Now that you've chosen your project, use this form to summarize your plans for it. It will help you clarify your focus.

1. Topic

    (a) My topic is

    (b) I chose this topic because

2. Purpose

    (a) The purpose of my piece is

    (b) I chose this purpose because

3. Audience

    (a) My audience is

    (b) I chose this audience because

4. Format

    (a) My format is

    (b) I chose this format because

    (c) It suits my topic because

    (d) It suits my purpose because

    (e) It suits my audience because

I Know, I Wonder

List the information you know about your topic under "What I Know." Then, for each point, think of a few questions you would like to answer. List the questions under "What I Wonder." Use another page if you need more space. When you are finished, consider all your questions and write a one-sentence answer to the question at the bottom of the page.

What I Know	What I Wonder

What do I want to find out about my topic?

I keep six honest serving men
(They taught me all I knew)
Their names are What and Why and When
and How and Where and Who

— RUDYARD KIPLING

Choose two questions about your topic for each category and write them in the boxes provided.

Who	When

What	Why

Where	How

Think About It

How is the skill of asking questions useful outside of the classroom?

Question Quotations

Read the following quotations about questions. How do they relate to your own experience in asking questions? Choose a quotation and write a one-page report about how it applies to your own experience.

"You start a question, and it's like starting a stone. You sit quietly on the top of a hill; and away the stone goes, starting others."

— ROBERT LOUIS STEVENSON

"You find the right answer by asking the right question."

— HINDU PROVERB

"A wise man's question contains half the answer."

— SOLOMON IBN GABIROL

"It's better to know some of the questions than all of the answers."

— JAMES THURBER

Think About It

Create your own quotation about questions. Write it above.

Classroom Questions

What does every researcher need? Questions! How does your classroom rate when it comes to questions? Work with your group to answer these questions about questions in your classroom. Be specific in your answers.

1. What are the most common types of questions asked in our classroom?

2. Why do we ask questions in our classroom?

3. Why are questions valuable?

4. When is it hard to ask good questions?

5. When is it easy to ask good questions?

6. Which kinds of questions result in interesting discussions?

7. How could we encourage more interesting questions?

Our recommendations for questions in the classroom are, as follows:

Questions, Questions, Questions

After your group has brainstormed questions on a specific topic, complete this form together.

1. How many questions were asked during the session?

2. Did the group run out of questions at any time? If so, what got it started again?

3. Was it easier to think of questions at the beginning of the session or at the end? Why do you think that was the case?

4. Was there a change in the type of questions asked from the beginning to the end of the session? Explain your answer with examples.

5. Did all group members have an opportunity to contribute questions? What support did group members offer each other to encourage more questions?

6. Which were the most interesting questions asked (List 3 to 5.)

7. What could your group have done differently to encourage even more interesting questions?

8. What would you say are the benefits of having a group brainstorm?

Three Types of Questions

There are many types of questions that can be asked. Three types are summarized below and examples given of each. Work with your group to create similar questions based on a chosen text. Leave the answers blank. When you are finished, exchange your list of questions with another group and answer the questions posed by that group.

Type 1: Questions with answers found "on" the lines

These are knowledge and comprehension questions. You can find the answers right in the text. For example: "What is the largest desert in the world?" "Why did the expedition turn back?"

a.   Question: b.   Question:

     Answer: Answer:

Type 2: Questions with answers found "between" the lines

These are sometimes called Search and Think questions. You can use clues from the text to determine the answer. For example: "If you had led the expedition, which supplies would you have taken?" "How was this expedition similar to the one the year before?

a.   Question: b.   Question:

     Answer: Answer:

Type 3: Questions with answers found "beyond" the lines

You need to use your prior knowledge or your ability to speculate to answer these kinds of questions: For example: "What might the explorer have written in his journal that night?" "Whose contribution was more important, that of the country's first prime minister, or that of the present prime minister?

a.   Question: b.   Question:

     Answer: Answer:

Group Dynamics

Use this page to record your observations of group skills and to assess your own contribution in a group setting.

1. Which of these roles did you observe group members taking? Underline the appropriate points.

   (a) reminding the group to stay on task
       Give an example:

   (b) contributing a variety of ideas
       Give an example:

   (c) asking for clarification or explanation of ideas
       Give an example:

   (d) giving credit to other members
       Give an example:

   (e) giving encouragement to other members
       Give an example:

   (f) helping to resolve differences and reach agreement
       Give an example:

   (g) moving the group along to the next stage
       Give an example:

   (h) using body language to show interest
       Give an example:

2. Answer these stems about your own contributions when you work in groups:

   (a) In a group discussion I tend to

   (b) I would like to improve my ability to

   (c) I could improve my participation in group work in these ways:

   (d) I could support and encourage other group members by

Using Research Skills

You have used research skills many times both in and out of the classroom. Think about your experiences while you answer these questions. Be specific in your answers.

1. How have you used research skills in Science?

2. How have you used research skills in Social Studies?

3. How have you used research skills in English?

4. How have you used research skills in Math?

5. How have you used research skills in Fine Arts?

6. How have you used research skills in other school subjects?

7. How have you used research skills in your daily life?

Think About It

What can you conclude about your research skills? Which skills are your strongest? Which would you like to improve?

Identifying Keywords

Keywords are important because they help you quickly and easily locate information. Use the steps outlined on this page to help you decide on keywords for your topic.

1. Phrase your topic in the form of a question:

2. List words, names, and abbreviations associated with your topic. Select nouns (naming words) rather than verbs (action words).

3. List synonyms and other spellings (such as colour, color) for words in step 1.

4. Do any of these words belong in phrases? (for example, "endangered animals" or "thermal energy")

5. Which groups or organizations might have information about your topic on their Web pages?

6. Which broader terms could apply to your topic?

7. Which topics with similar words are unrelated to your topic? (for example, "marshmallow" versus "marsh mellow")

8. List all your keywords here:

Electronic Equipment Checklist

Which electronic equipment have you used? Put a check in one of the two columns on the right. Circle the name of any equipment that you have access to at school or at home. How would you best describe the equipment's purpose?

Type of Equipment	Description of Purpose	Have you used this technology?	
		Yes	Not Yet
printer			
scanner			
digital camera			
camcorder			
CD-ROM			
DVD			
keyboard			
FAX			
VCR			
copy machine			
overhead projector			
slide projector			
television			
tape recorder			
telephone			
video editor			
calculator			

Other equipment I can use:

Computer Functions Checklist

Which computer functions have you already had occasion to use? Put a check in one of the three columns for each function.

	I haven't needed to use this yet	I know a little about it	I know how to use it
File			
save as different file type			
access Help			
copy file			
move file			
delete file			
preview pages for printing			
alter print features (landscape/portrait)			
Edit			
find/change			
copy and paste data in new file			
Insert			
insert table or graph from another document			
insert clip art			
insert video clips			
insert page number			
insert page break			
Format			
text alignment			
font size			
font type			
font style			
headers			
footers			
margins			
columns			
create a new folder			
create a new file			
double-space document			
create columns			
use bullets			
create border			
create shading			
Tools			
thesaurus			
spell check			
grammar check			
use word count			

Spreadsheet Functions Checklist

Which of the computer functions listed below have you already used?
Put a check in one of the three columns for each function.

	I haven't needed to use this yet	I know a little about it	I know how to use it
open, save, and locate files			
move cell pointer			
print and alter print features			
enter labels/numbers			
cut, copy, paste, insert, type over cell contents			
create and modify charts			

calculations
   sum
   average
   count
   minimum
   maximum			

format cells			
access Help			
use sort functions			

Think About It

What would you like to learn next about using spreadsheet functions?

Part B:

The Search for Information

Chapter 4

Identify and Evaluate Sources, Materials, and Tools

Identify Sources and Materials

FROM THE GENERAL TO THE SPECIFIC

Objective: to identify primary and secondary resources

Skills at Work: analysing, classifying, deciding, evaluating, identifying

Activity: class and pairs discussion, BLM: Primary and Secondary Source Checklist (p. 103)

Display an autobiography and a biography about the same person. Ask students: What is the difference between these two formats? (A biography is written about the life of someone other that the author; an autobiography is written about one's self.) Introduce the terms *primary* and *secondary*. **Primary research** (autobiography) involves going right to the source for information (interview, survey, direct observation). A primary source could be a person or something a person has created, such as a speech, letters, or diary. **Secondary research** (biography) involves using what someone else has said about the source. A secondary source could be a book, film, CD-ROM, or magazine.

Have a variety of resources on hand and discuss each with the class, asking whether it is a primary or secondary source of information. Then ask students to discuss in pairs, "Which should be done first — primary or secondary research? And why?" Students can identify several points in favor of each possible answer and decide which should come first. Take a tally of students' responses, or have students divide into two teams based on their answers and debate their positions. Make sure students note that secondary research often needs to precede primary since it provides the background knowledge to appreciate the primary. Primary research helps to bring a subject alive. Encourage students to include primary research in their research plan. Lessons on how to gather primary research can be found in Chapter 5, Access Information.

To reinforce their understanding, you could direct students to complete BLM: Primary and Secondary Source Checklist.

Plug It In: Ask students to respond to this question: Does the Internet provide access to primary or to secondary sources? (The answer is both.) Students could identify several sites for each category and explain how they made their decision.

Objective: *to identify personal
skills*

Skills at Work: *celebrating,
identifying, summarizing,
synthesizing*

Activity: *partner interview,
creation of advertisement*

Everyone is an authority on something! Ask students to interview partners about their skills, knowledge, and experiences. First, they can develop a list of general questions designed to draw out the information on topics such as lessons taken, reports researched, special experiences, and talents. Next, they can interview a partner and record the responses, asking follow-up questions to check understanding. Let the partners switch roles.

Now it's time for each student to create an advertisement for their partner, describing their area of expertise. Have students consider the elements of an effective advertisement, such as clear, persuasive text and eye-catching design. They could use Help Wanted ads from the classified or career sections of local newspapers as models, analysing the use of words, phrases, and slogans, and assessing the impact of font and style. Encourage students to use figurative language, such as alliteration, as well as specific nouns and vivid verbs, in creating their own persuasive messages.

Students should also consider these two questions in designing their ads: Who will the audience be? Where will the ads be placed? Have them consider how they can revise their wording. Graphics representing the skills can be used, and students should choose colors based on appeal.

Consider posting the ads in the classroom for students to refer to when they need help.

Take It Further: If students need to locate authorities on a topic within the school community, they could put up Help Wanted advertisements in the school. Students could describe their projects or areas of research and advertise for the particular kind of help they want. The Help Wanted ads could be placed on bulletin boards or on the school's Web site, or read aloud as announcements. Students could brainstorm other ways of identifying sources within the school (such as creating and distributing questionnaires or conducting a survey) and follow up on them if the prospects seem good.

**HUMAN SOURCES OF
INFORMATION**

Objective: *to identify authorities
in the community*

Skills at Work: *generating,
identifying, summarizing,
synthesizing*

Activity: *group brainstorm*

Sometimes the best source of information is a resource person. How can students identify authorities outside of the school? Groups of students can brainstorm this question. Remind students that they will probably know some experts, such as friends, relatives, and community elders. Their brainstorming session should consider how to identify both authorities they know and those they have not met. Students could refer to phone books, community newspapers and magazines, community resource directories, or Web sites for ideas. Then groups can revise and organize their lists and identify possible ways to contact the authorities (by phone, fax, e-mail, personal visits). Groups can report to the class. You may want to combine this lesson with "Resource Comparison" later in this chapter and discuss the credibility of sources.

Plug It In: Have students identify useful Web sites and e-mail addresses for authorities in the fields of current projects. They could ask a chat group or discussion group (listserver type), USENET newsgroup, or people finders (much like on-line phone books) to direct them.

CLASSROOM RESOURCES

Objective: *to identify where and how classroom resources are located*

Skills at Work: *classifying, deciding, identifying, organizing*

Activity: *categorizing*

Choose several books that could be placed in various categories. (For example, ocean creatures could be in a section on ocean, on animals, or on photography.) Ask students for their suggestions about which category each should be grouped in. There is no right or wrong answer. Let them present reasons for their choices and discover that there could be several appropriate categories for each selection.

Discuss how nonfiction books are arranged in the classroom. Where would students find a book about . . . ? Where would they find encyclopedias or other general references? Where are the dictionaries kept? What suggestions do students have for how all the books should be categorized? Small groups could be in charge of each category and check for books that should be elsewhere.

Students currently working on a research project could complete BLM: Classroom Resources (p. 104) for their topics.

HOW TO FIND LIBRARY RESOURCES

Objective: *to gain familiarity with Dewey decimal classification*

Skills at Work: *analysing, classifying, identifying*

Activity: *library exploration*

You might wish to use this lesson before the class pays a visit to a library. See also the following lesson, "Library Orientation."

Before students visit the library to search for nonfiction books, they need to have an understanding of the Dewey decimal classification system. You can explain to them that this system was created more than a hundred years ago by Melvin Dewey. In his time, some libraries organized their books by date purchased or by book size. Why would these systems be difficult to use? Dewey devised a system of classifying books based on ten classes, each with ten divisions, which are further broken down into ten sections. For example, the class Science, 500, is broken into these divisions:

500 Science
510 Mathematics
520 Astronomy
530 Physics
540 Chemistry
550 Earth science
560 Paleontology

570 Life sciences
580 Botany
590 Zoology

Each division is broken down into ten sections which are further broken down by decimals. For example, a book about horses would be classed as follows:

The class 600 is Technology.
The division 630 is Agriculture.
The section 636 is Domestic Animals.
The decimal designation 636.1 is Horses.

Each nonfiction book is assigned a specific call number. Advise students that they do not need to memorize categories; they simply need to look up the call number in the catalogue and locate the book on the shelf. Remind them that fiction books are not numbered, but are arranged alphabetically by the author's last name. Some libraries have separate sections for Mysteries, Science Fiction, Westerns, Fantasy, and so on. Most public libraries have separate sections for Young Adult fiction, Juvenile fiction, and Early readers.

For students' reference, you may want to distribute Appendix 2, Dewey Decimal Classification System. Have students make guesses about the categories in which books on their topic might be found, then compare those guesses with their library searches. Students can also choose a category they are unfamiliar with and browse the shelves, looking for interesting books within that section.

LIBRARY ORIENTATION

Objective: *to identify resources in library*

Skills at Work: *classifying, deciding, identifying, integrating, organizing*

Activity: *library visit and mapping, blackline master work (see pp. 105, 106)*

Before your class visits the library, you might wish to review classification of nonfiction books by referring to the previous lesson, "How to Find Library Resources." Students could take a tour through the library and note the locations of various sections. Students who are familiar with the library could act as tour guides for other students or begin work on BLM: Library Scavenger Hunt. Then students could draw maps, roughly to scale of the floor plan of the library, showing the locations of the sections. They should include and label the fiction sections and the nonfiction resources, including vertical files, librarians' desks, audio-visual materials, computer terminals, card catalogue, and periodicals (newspapers and magazines). Students can use BLM: Library Checklist to make sure they have found all the sections.

After students have familiarized themselves with the layout, they can work with a partner to complete BLM: Library Scavenger Hunt. Advanced searchers could spend time examining the volumes in the reference collection, including the various indexes, such as reader's guides to periodicals.

Plug It In: Ask students to consider how the Internet and a library are similar. What makes them different? Let students work in small groups to identify criteria, such as the amount and type of resources, ease of access, and organization, and summarize their results in a compare/contrast chart or Venn diagram. A sample compare/contrast chart appears nearby. Your students might evaluate those categories in a different way or suggest different categories.

Internet and Library Resources: A Compare/Contrast Chart

	Internet	Library
Availability	24 hours a day, 365 days a year	limited hours
Amount of Resources	limitless	limited by budget and space
Type of Resources	wide variety	limited by collection policies
Reliability of Resources	very poor—sites may disappear, information is questionable	excellent, though may be outdated
Ease of Use	can be frustrating and time consuming	straightforward; librarian can help

Evaluate Sources and Materials

RESOURCE EVALUATION

Objective: to evaluate nonfiction books

Skills: analysing, evaluating, speculating

Activity: discussion

Ask students to share their experiences researching: Have they selected resources that were too hard to understand or that didn't have the right information? What do they suggest doing differently next time? How can they tell if a book will be a good source? What do they look for?

Prompt students to speculate on the qualities of an ideal resource book or other resource format. They can represent their answers in the form of an invitation ("Come and meet the ideal resource book . . .") and include sample "pages" from their imaginary book (maybe the table of contents and index), adding captions and labels to show the features that make it easy to use.

You might want to distribute Strategy Spotlight: Evaluating a Nonfiction Book, page 90, for students' reference. Students can follow the steps to evaluate library or other materials.

RESOURCE COMPARISON

Objective: to compare news coverage

Skills at Work: analysing, evaluating, integrating, synthesizing

Activity: studying media

Ask students if they agree with this quotation by Friedrich Nietzsche:

"There are no facts, only interpretations."

Explore with them why they agree or disagree with it. Students can speculate on what might have prompted the philosopher to make this statement. Do they have any experiences or observations that support his statement?

Invite students to suggest recent news stories and select one. Then ask group members to monitor how the story is treated in two of the same media, such as two TV news casts from different stations, two magazines, two newspapers, or two Internet news sites. Direct them to identify and summarize similarities and differences in presentation and content and speculate how the differences might alter the perception of the reader or viewer. Here are some questions they might explore: What's fact? What's opinion? Are there any words that indicate bias? If so, which ones? Do you prefer one version to the other? Why? Have you changed your reaction to Nietzsche's statement as a result of this activity? Groups can meet again in several days to compare their results: what was similar or different in the news coverage between electronic and print sources?

Do It Differently: Direct students to write stories in which the last line is "There are no facts, only interpretations." They can first outline their plots and consider their choice for characters and setting.

Take It Further: Have students compare a book and its video version, or two versions of the same story (such as a myth or fairy tale) by two different authors. Ask them to note what stayed the same and what changed, and speculate about the reasons for the change. Did the changes improve the story? Why or why not? They can chart their responses on a compare/contrast chart or Venn diagram or summarize their observations in paragraph form. Students could also write their own versions of common tales, then exchange and compare.

Plug It In: Invite students to compare print and electronic media. In which version would they rather read a letter? a news article? a book? Why? Which version would they rather use for writing a letter? a news article? a book? Why?

ADVERTISEMENT ANALYSIS

Objective: to increase awareness of ads

Skills at Work: analysing, evaluating, identifying, speculating

Activity: class and small group brainstorming

Can an advertisement be a useful source of information? Ask students to respond to this question with specific examples of advertisements they have seen, heard, or read. Then pose this question: Is advertising good or bad? Ask for students' opinions, backed up by their experiences. You might wish to tally votes for each position. What conclusions can be drawn from the results of the votes? Ask students to consider what is advertising and what is not. For example, is a label inside a sweater advertising? Why or why not? What about a label on the outside of a sweater? As a class, brainstorm formats that are used for advertising.

Have students break into small groups and discuss what advertising they have observed in the school. What's being sold and why? This activity could become a competition between groups as to which can name the greatest number of school advertisements in ten minutes. Groups should be prepared to defend all their choices when they present their lists to the class. They can also consider why each item is being advertised in the school. Students could debate whether corporate ads should be displayed in any form in the school.

Think About It: Mark Twain coined this expression: "Many a small thing has been made large by the right kind of advertising." Invite students to make a journal entry to explore the author's comment. Do they agree or disagree with it? What evidence have they seen in their own lives of how publicity has made the importance of something greater? Are they surprised by the results? Do ads become less visible when there are many of them? What conclusions can they draw from their observations?

Take It Further: Ask students to analyse the ads they see, read, or hear for a whole day, recording their observations about the format, location, and purpose of each ad.

FACT VERSUS OPINION

Objective: *to distinguish between fact and opinion*

Skills at Work: *analysing, deciding, evaluating*

Activity: *discussion, BLM: Fact and Opinion (p. 107), game creation*

Name a topic and ask one student for a fact about it, and another student for an opinion about it. Then have other students make statements without saying whether they are facts or opinions. How easy is it for students to identify which they are? Work together to create a class definition of "fact" and "opinion." You could ask students to complete BLM: Fact and Opinion for reinforcement. Let them share their answers with classmates and give each other feedback about whether the facts are facts and the opinions are opinions.

Encourage students to review writing they are doing for their project, or other samples they have done. Have they expressed one opinion, several opinions, or all sides of issues? Did they include facts that support different points of view, even when trying to persuade the reader of one point of view?

Do It Differently: Pairs of students can create Fact or Opinion games, using a simple board game or card game format. The games might involve identifying a statement as fact or opinion, or requiring the player to make a fact or opinion statement about a topic.

Take It Further: Take a few minutes after reading information aloud to the class, or after watching videos, to discuss the author's opinion and point of view. Were all sides of the issue given equal weight? What signs of bias could students detect? Is the author trying to gain something through the writing?

MAGAZINES AS SOURCES

Objective: *to evaluate magazines*

Skills at Work: *analysing, evaluating, identifying, summarizing*

Activity: *studying magazines*

Direct students to bring in a copy of their favorite magazine or a magazine they think would be useful as a research source. Ask them what criteria they use to judge magazines. Have students give a brief oral review of their choices, analysing areas such as content, pictures, layout, and use of color (or other criteria that the class identifies). Alternatively, students could write a paragraph about their choice and display the summary with their magazine for other students to read. They could also complete this sentence stem, "If I could change one thing about this magazine, it would be _____ because _____." You might wish to have on hand a variety of magazines from the library for students to assess, such as *National Geographic*, *Equinox*, *Yes*, and *Smithsonian*.

Take It Further: If students are currently working on a research project, have them design a magazine cover or cover story about their topic. They can model their pieces on the magazine they chose earlier, incorporating similar design features, colors, and layout.

Identify and Evaluate Tools

Place the word "Technology" in a circle on the board. Ask students to brainstorm words, ideas, and opinions that come to mind when they think of technology, and group their responses to form a web. Then ask students to name their favorite invention of recent years. Encourage them to share the reasons for their choices and examples of how the inventions have enriched their lives. Discuss why people make inventions.

Next, ask students to list technology used to transmit and receive data (computers, fax machines, telephones, television, video players, digital cameras, and so on). Write their responses on the board in a tally chart. Using a show of hands, tally the number of students who know how to use each medium. Ask, "What advantages are there for being able to send and receive electronic messages to other parts of the world?"

Then have students work in small groups to complete BLM: Compare and Contrast Technologies.

Do It Differently: Ask students to estimate the number of hours each week their family uses media, such as computers, television, and radio. They can record their total estimates and their estimates for each medium. Have students keep a record of one week's media consumption by category. Then share and compare responses, creating a class chart of number of hours per medium. What conclusions can be drawn? Which medium receives the most use? Which has the least? How would students define spending "too much time" with electronic media? Ask them what else they enjoy doing with their free time.

Plug It In: Challenge advanced students to compare and contrast analog and digital technology, which are defined in the Glossary.

Think About It: What changes in technology do students anticipate experiencing in their lifetimes? Invite students to explore this question with a journal entry, predicting the types and results of changes they expect to see. When might these changes happen? In five years? In 50 years?

Take It Further: Which technological improvements have grandparents and community elders seen in their lifetimes? Invite students to interview older relatives and friends to discover which inventions they find the most useful. Which modern inventions do they find unnecessary? How have inventions changed their workplaces and lifestyles? Students can share their research with classmates and note similarities and differences in the responses. You may wish to distribute Strategy Spotlight: Interview Tips and Techniques, page 93, to help students formulate and conduct interviews.

**THE INTERNET AS A
RESOURCE**

Objective: *to identify Internet use*

Skills at Work: *evaluating,
generating*

Activity: *class discussion, group
work*

Ask students: What have you used the Internet for? Students can share their experiences researching, playing games, sending and receiving e-mail, publishing their work, creating Web sites, and so on. Record the categories of their responses on the board, then ask them to speculate what percentage of Internet users use each category.

(A study in the *Wall Street Journal* in December 1999 found these percentages for people who used the Internet at least once a month: e-mail 96 per cent, using search engines 88 per cent, researching products and services 72 per cent, reading news 51 per cent, online chat 45 per cent.)

The following statistics show the length of time it took for various technologies to reach 30 per cent of the population. Share these statistics with the class, either by using an overhead projector or by writing them on the board.

telephone — 38 years
television — 17 years
personal computer — 13 years
Internet — 7 years

Source: Morgan Stanley Research Group 1999 from U.S. Internet Council

Ask students to consider what factors might explain why the Internet has penetrated the market faster than the other technologies. Is the Internet more or less important than the other technologies? When is it the best way to search for information? What are the strengths and weaknesses for searching? Have students consider these questions in small groups and summarize their ideas. Then these groups can form larger groups and make a master summary. The large group summaries can be compared and a class list created and posted.

Some of the following ideas will probably emerge. The Internet is preferred when information needs to be up to date, when basic, factual information, such as addresses or statistics, is sought, when there's not much information available in the library, and when a researcher would like to correspond with an expert. The Internet might not be as good for in-depth or specialized research or copyrighted material that exists in print. Since a search can take a long time and much of the material found may be of questionable authority, the Internet is not always a good choice when a researcher has little time.

Plug It In: Have students find out the current number of people online in various countries around the world. They can create graphs or tables of their findings, showing differences by country, age group, and so on. Some useful online resources for this research include NUA Internet Surveys, CyberAtlas, and Nielsen Net Ratings.

Students could also create their own survey regarding the amount or type of Internet use. The survey could be posted on the school Web site or sent out to keypals or other schools.

Think About It: Invite students to make a journal entry to explore their thoughts about the effect that the Internet might have on the gap between rich and poor nations. How many people in the world can afford high technology hardware and software?

Take It Further: Start a class collection of favorite Internet sites. The information can be shared in a group folder, along with a brief explanation of who recommended the site, the date, and the site's special features.

INTERNET USE

Objective: _to identify Internet challenges_

Skills at Work: _evaluating, generating, identifying, predicting, problem solving_

Activity: _group discussion_

Ask students to brainstorm answers to this question: What are some challenges of searching on the Net? Answers might include Web sites coming and going, difficulty in deciding keywords, distraction, downloading time, and false information. Write this sentence stem on the board: "The Internet would be easier and better to use if . . ."

Small groups could discuss how they would complete this stem, then represent their ideas on a chart, grouping their answers into categories (such as difficulties navigating, identifying, and evaluating). These charts could be posted and form the basis for other lessons about using the Internet effectively. Some students may be able to identify solutions to difficulties and teach peers how to overcome them. Advice on overcoming Internet challenges can be found in the next two lessons and in Chapter 5, Access Information.

Plug It In: Do students find it challenging to locate the photos, pictures, or graphics they want on the Internet? Search engines have limitations. They look for terms or file names and so might not locate the images even though they are out there. Students could try searching museum or art gallery sites, and note filename extensions, such as **.jpg** or **.gif**. Start a class collection of good sources for graphics, cartoons, symbols, etc.

Think About It: Do students to make a journal entry to explore what having limitless access to information means to them. How might the Internet influence their lives and future careers? Which issues of personal privacy do they speculate becoming a problem?

Take It Further: Start a class glossary of technology words and their definitions. Refer students to specialized print or electronic dictionaries, such as those in Recommended Resources at the end of this book.

Objective: *to identify Internet search tools*

Skills at Work: *classifying, evaluating, generating, problem solving, speculating*

Activity: *class discussion*

Prompt students to describe steps of how they search for information on the Internet. After a number of methods have been described (search engines, subject directories, browsing, typing in URLs), then ask: Why are there so many ways to search the Internet? Has anyone ever actually searched the Internet? (This is a trick question: no one actually could search the Internet. When you use a search tool, you are searching a database about other databases and Web pages.) What problems have students encountered using search engines and subject directories? Make a list on the board. What hints or shortcuts can students offer about the problems?

You might wish to make a class collection of hints and solutions to search problems as a reference for students. The information could be stored electronically or as a poster that could be added to from time to time as students encounter new problems or new solutions.

Distribute Strategy Spotlight: Electronic Search Tools, page 91, and review it with the class. Students might wish to review and recommend their favorite search tools. See if they can identify those tools as search engines or subject directories. Remind students that although it is helpful to know about search tools, it's the students' ability to think and evaluate that really matters.

Notes: For activities evaluating Web sites, see the next lesson, "Internet Evaluation Forms." For activities on phrasing keywords, see "Boolean Logic" in Chapter 5, Access Information, and "Keywords Focus" in Chapter 3, Create a Plan.

Plug It In: Ask students to share their response to this question: Why should you explore different categories from the same subject directory? Students can explain their answers to partners, or write a paragraph in response. Ensure they understand that no one subject directory includes all the information available and that each has its own way of categorizing information and identifying keywords.

Think About It: Could a new tool that could always find all the information on a subject anywhere on the Internet be invented? How might the tool work? Invite students to explore these ideas through a journal entry.

INTERNET EVALUATION FORMS

Objective: to evaluate Web sites

Skills at Work: analysing, deciding, evaluating, identifying, integrating, problem solving

Activity: evaluation form creation

In order to have time to complete both parts of this lesson, you might wish to use several class sessions.

PART ONE

Write this statement on the board (you may wish to underline "anyone" and "anything"): Anyone can publish anything on the Web. Ask students to name the advantages of anyone publishing. Then ask for disadvantages, and list them on the board. The disadvantages could lead to a discussion of the need to evaluate Web sites for their content, accuracy, presentation, and ease of navigation. For each disadvantage listed, consider developing criteria for evaluation.

Tell students to work in small groups to create their own Web site evaluation forms. They can use the criteria identified and include any other factors they consider important for judging sites. Suggest that their forms include a system of ranking a site for each of the criteria. Groups can compare their forms, noting similarities and differences, and adding any additional points they wish. A sample form is provided on BLM: Web Site Evaluation Form (p. 109).

If time permits, students can visit some Web sites you have bookmarked or listed in advance. Ask them to rank each site, including their ideas of how the low scoring sites could be improved. If there is not sufficient time, this activity can be assigned to be completed in the next few days.

Plug It In: There is a lot of information available on the Internet about Web site evaluation. Students can research other examples of Web site evaluation forms and compare them with their own. Is there anything they'd like to change or add to theirs?

PART TWO

With the class, read and discuss Strategy Spotlight: Is It the Right Site?, page 92. You might wish to expand your discussion to include evaluation of all information. Distribute BLM: Web Users, Beware! (p. 110). Ask students to share their experiences noticing these triggers. How did they respond? Students can create signs to post at computer stations in the classroom and at home to remind users to beware.

Sources, Materials, and Tools

OUTSTANDING RESOURCES

Objective: *to identify useful resources*

Skills at Work: *celebrating, deciding, evaluating, generating, identifying*

Activity: *award creation*

What is the best information source students have used? Have they found an excellent Web site or reference book? Is there an encyclopedia, CD-ROM, local expert, or news station they think deserves an award? Students can choose sources and prepare a written summary of reasons for their choice. Then they can make a Resource of the Year Award. The awards can be beautifully decorated and should include an explanation, such as "This Resource of the Year Award is given to _____ because of _____ as shown by _____." Invite students to make choices about the size, type, and style of lettering to use. The finished awards can be displayed in the classroom as recommendations to other students.

Take It Further: Students can submit or present their awards (or letters detailing their reasons) to the people who produced the resources.

RESOURCE CHECKLIST

Objective: *to identify sources*

Skills at Work: *classifying, generating, identifying, organizing, summarizing*

Activity: *completion of blackline masters The Search and Resource Checklist (pp. 111, 112)*

The blackline masters The Search and Resource Checklist can be used for students undertaking a research project. If students don't have a project currently assigned, they could complete a mini-project on a career of interest, using these blackline masters to track their research.

Student Self-Assessment

Ask students to identify their strengths in finding and evaluating electronic and non-electronic resources. Which skills would they like to improve? What steps could they take to strengthen their skills? How will they evaluate their skills? Students can record their goals for future reference and refinement.

Chapter 5

Access Information

Access Human Resources

EFFECTIVE INTERVIEWING

Objective: *to identify interview techniques*

Skills at Work: *collaborating, deciding, generating, integrating, observing, synthesizing*

Activity: *group discussion, debate, BLM: Change the Questions (p. 113)*

What is more important in an interview — the questions or the answers? Ask students to consider their answer to this question, then form into two groups based on responses. The groups can discuss together the reasons for their responses and create a summary chart listing the strong points in favor of their opinion. This activity can evolve into a debate; alternatively, each group can report on their findings and students can follow up by writing with an increased appreciation for the other point of view.

Find out what tips students can share about how to conduct a successful interview. Summarize students' points on the board. Prompt them with questions about how they could practise their interviewing skills and whether they have observed professional interviewers on TV. What types of body language show a listener is listening attentively? What qualities do the best interviewers display? What is the advantage of going right to the source for information? To provide a summary of ideas, distribute Strategy Spotlight: Interview Tips and Techniques, page 93. For practice in formulating questions that ask for more than a yes/no answer, direct students to complete BLM: Change the Questions.

Take It Further: Students can practise formulating questions about nonfiction that they have read. What questions would they ask the author about the topic? Ask students to review their own writing and think of questions their readers might have. Tell them to assess whether their writing answers the questions.

TELEPHONE ACCESS

Objective: *to review telephone skills and manners*

Skills at Work: *analysing, identifying, predicting, synthesizing*

Activity: *phone book search, discussion*

What experience have students had using a phone book? Ask them to share the difficulties and successes they have had searching for listings. Depending on students' skill levels, you may want to first review alphabetical order, then have students find the listings in the phone book for their family or friends, the school, and a neighborhood recreation complex (swimming pool, skating rink, or movie theatre).

Have the students discover the type and purpose of listings in each section of the phone book. Where are the government listings found? How are they organized? Which listings are in the white pages? How are they organized? Which listings are in the yellow pages? How are they organized? You may wish to prepare a list of government, residential, and business names and have students practise finding the listings.

Discuss phone manners and why they are important. How do they help a researcher? If students will be phoning for information as part of a research project, have them prepare a script of how the phone call might go. They should clearly identify who they are, why they are calling, and who they wish to speak to. They should also limit their questions to two or three unless they have arranged for more time in advance.

Plug It In: Have students find phone numbers on the Internet using search engines or subject directories. Students can use an electronic folder to collect useful site addresses for locating phone numbers.

Take It Further: Have students work individually or in pairs to brainstorm answers to these questions: Where else is alphabetical order used to organize information? What are some other ways of organizing information? Alternatively, students can find examples in the classroom or at home to answer the above questions (such as a recipe book organized by category or a biography arranged chronologically).

INFORMATION REQUESTS

Objective: *to write effective letters*

Skills at Work: *identifying, organizing*

Activity: *letter writing*

Is there a project the students are working on that could involve writing letters? Ask students to suggest what points should be included in formal letters or requests for information (who you are, what you want, why you want it, when you need it). Remind students to be polite and appreciative, to recognize that the correspondent is taking time to respond, and to be specific in what they request. For example, "send me everything you have about China" may not result in their receiving the map of the Great Wall that they want. Once students have drafted letters, the letters should be checked over for language use, grammar, spelling, and punctuation. If they're using the common block format it is unnecessary to indent paragraphs, just leave a space between them. Advise them to close letters with Sincerely or Yours truly. Since it can take a number of weeks to receive a written response, students should proceed with other types of research for their projects.

Take It Further: Invite students to design their own letterhead for use in writing business letters. Their choice of font, size, style, and type should make their information easy to understand and business-like in appearance.

Plug It In: If students are sending their requests by e-mail, ask them to identify aspects of effective e-mail messages, such as using short paragraphs and carefully proofreading the message (perhaps using spell check). Ask them to consider what might be the advantages and disadvantages of sending an e-mail message rather than a letter.

A survey is a means of conducting primary research to determine opinions, preferences, or other information. It does not go as deeply into responses as does a focus group or personal interview, but it is a useful way to find out what a group of people think about an issue or idea. It is also a good activity for improving skill in selecting variables, such as the type and wording of questions, and the selection and number of respondents.

Find examples of surveys and survey results in newspapers, magazines, Web sites, and so on. Alternatively, call upon students to bring in examples. Some magazines and news stations have ongoing viewer polls posted at their Web sites. Discuss what a sample is (a representation of the population surveyed to determine how the rest of the population thinks or feels), and how samples might be selected.

Examine the survey questions. Are they multiple choice, ranking, or open-ended? Clear, unambiguous questions are essential for a successful survey. Are there leading questions (questions formulated to lead the respondent to a particular answer)? Discuss how to read the results. Objective questions, using multiple choice or ranking answers, are easier to tabulate and interpret. Subjective questions, using open-ended answers (how do you feel . . .), are more difficult to tabulate and represent.

Provide students with BLM: Survey Plan so that they can plan their own surveys. Working with a partner or a group on a survey helps to share the work and improve the quality of the questions.

Plug It In: Students can extend their survey electronically to include students at other schools. They can graph the results, analyse their data, infer, and draw conclusions.

Take It Further: Integrate math activities into survey studies. Have students determine percentages and graph or chart the survey results.

Discuss with students the value of listening skills both in and out of the classroom. Ask students to identify careers where listening skills are especially valuable (musician, teacher, reporter). Bring out the connection between listening and attention. How can listening skills help the research process? You might wish to discuss how attention is important to a person with limited or no hearing.

ARE YOU LISTENING?

Ask students to work in pairs or small groups. Students can take turns sharing some information that is important to them, perhaps their view on a current issue, a special event they attended, or a holiday they took. Other group members should use body language to show they are not interested (look away, yawn, act bored, and so on). After each member has had a chance, discuss their experiences. Then repeat the activity with a new topic of interest. This time group members can show interest through their body language (listening attentively, nodding, making eye contact, and so on). Again, discuss experiences.

WHAT DID YOU SAY?

Choose a topic for students to express their opinions about. Ask them, one by one, to express their views and a reason or example to back them up. Here's the catch: each student must first paraphrase the statements of the previous student before expressing his or her own opinion.

DID YOU HEAR THAT?

Have students number off into four groups. Assign each a category. Read aloud a list of words and ask students to write down the words that belong in their category. Then they can meet in their groups and compare lists. Adapt the sample word list below to feature information currently being studied in the classroom. The words in this list include some that might fit more than one category. To make the activity easier, use simple words and categories.

Categories: Ecosystems, Solar System, Energy, Geology

habitat	planet	temperature	rock
species	meteor	heat	mineral
black hole	generator	fossils	organism
crystal	adaptation	star	magnet
erosion	climate	atmosphere	moon
sound	metal	comet	electricity

Access Print and Electronic Resources

CITING SOURCES

Objective: *to identify importance of citing resources*

Skills at Work: *classifying, generating, identifying, organizing*

Activity: *group work*

Have students form into groups to consider these questions: Can you use information exactly as you've copied it from the Internet? Is it the same or different than copying from a book? Do you have to tell the source, and if so, how do you do it? Which information do you have to include for each type of source? Students can use graphic organizers or charts to record and organize their ideas. Each group can exchange charts with another group and consider their points — is there anything they wish to add to or change on their own summary? Direct groups to exchange their charts with other groups until all groups have considered all reports. Then the class can discuss together and create an Internet use policy for the classroom and a bibliographic citation poster or chart for all types of resources. Students will find a basic format for recording resources on BLM: Recording Resources (p. 115). Advanced students may review Strategy Spotlight: How to Write a Bibliography, page 94.

BOOLEAN LOGIC

Objective: *to create more precise searches*

Skills at Work: *analysing, classifying, deciding, evaluating, synthesizing*

Activity: *Venn diagrams*

You may wish to refer to "Keywords Focus" in Chapter 3, Create a Plan, and "Search Tools" in Chapter 4, Identify and Evaluate Sources, Materials, and Tools. Ask students to consider their search strategies for the following topics:

1. Suppose they wanted to find Web pages with information about both wolves and coyotes. How would they enter their keywords? (**wolves and coyotes**)

2. Suppose they wanted pages that mentioned either wolves or coyotes. How would they enter their keywords? (**wolves or coyotes**)

3. Suppose they wanted pages that mentioned wolves, but did not mention coyotes. How would they enter their keywords? (**wolves not coyotes**)

Then explain that this system (called Boolean logic) works with many search engines and is a useful way to narrow a search. Demonstrate, or ask students to generate, a series of three Venn diagrams. One circle is labelled "wolves" and the other "coyotes." Shade in the appropriate sections for each scenario. (In wolves *and* coyotes, shade where the circles intersect. In wolves *or* coyotes, shade each side of the circles, but not where they intersect. In wolves, *not* coyotes, shade only the wolves side, and not where they intersect.) Have students work with their topic keywords using Boolean logic. The "or" designation can be helpful when searching for synonyms. The "not" can be helpful if there is a similar term with a different meaning (such as "army ant" specifying not military).

Strategy Spotlight: Can't Find What You Want on the Web?, page 95, offers students other helpful hints for searching.

Plug It In: Students can research the Help functions of their favorite search engines and discover which use Boolean logic. Ask them to find out what techniques the others use.

Review the parts of a book with students. Ask them to take out a textbook and find the pages outlined below. Stop at each page a moment and discuss what information can be found there. Encourage students to share their questions or frustrations using each of these pages, as well as their recommendations for when to use them. A few suggested questions are provided. Adapt these questions to suit the skill levels of your students.

1. *Title Page*
   Who is the author?

2. *Copyright Page*
   What year was this book published?
   Who are the publishers?
   In what city are the publishers located?

3. *Table of Contents*
   What is the name of Chapter 3?
   On what page does Chapter 7 begin?
   How many chapters are there altogether?
   Which chapters deal with . . . ?

4. *Index*
   On what page(s) would you find information about . . . ?

You may wish to have students scan through certain chapters, noticing the features, such as headings, photographs, charts, captions, and so on. Explore with them how the organization of the chapter helps readers find the information they need.

You might want to distribute Strategy Spotlight: Using Print Resources, page 96, to guide students as they access information.

Q & A GAMES

Objective: *to practise accessing information*

Skills at Work: *collaborating, deciding, locating, problem solving*

Activity: *information games*

FIND THE ANSWER

Have students create a question and an answer about a current topic of study. Each should be written on a separate piece of paper. Collect the questions in one pile and the answers in another in a mixed order. Every student gets an answer pinned or taped to their back and a question taped to their front. Then students can intermingle and find the answer to the question they are wearing.

TEAM RESEARCH

Teams of students can create questions on a topic currently under study, then exchange with other teams who find the answers in classroom resources. Discuss with students in advance that they will have to make decisions about where to look for information. Would it be faster for all group members to look for the same answer? Should they split up the questions? After they have found the answers, discuss what they could improve in their strategies next time.

ANSWER AND QUESTION

Set up a reference area with one or more sources of information about a topic under current study. Write a question that can be answered from the reference(s). Students can take turns coming to the area while other activities are going on. The first student answers the question, then creates a new question that can be answered from the resource. The next student answers that question, then adds a new question, and so on.

  BLM: Encyclopedias (p. 116) allows students to practise encyclopedia skills.

Student Self-Assessment

Have students consider their skills in accessing human, print, electronic, and Internet resources. Which skills would they like to improve? Students can formulate goals and ways to measure their success. The goals should be reviewed and refined from time to time as more skill is gained.

Chapter 6

Make Sense of Information

Observation Strategies

Encourage students to become more observant and to think about and make sense of their observations. Try some of these activities:

- Recommend that students carry notebooks with them at all times to record observations, connections to their projects, questions, and ideas.
- Have students "secretly" shadow each other for the day, making observations. They can then write up a character sketch and other students can guess who they are describing.
- Have students take jot notes on field trips, speculating on interesting historical figures, artifacts, and past or future lifestyles.
- Whenever appropriate, encourage students to use a number of senses — what did the air smell like? What looked different in the halls this morning? What sounds did they hear on the way to school?

Think About It: Invite students to make a journal entry to explore their answers to this question: How can you increase your skills in observing the results of an experiment or field research?

Reading Strategies

Ask students: When I assign a chapter to read, how do you do it? How many start at the beginning and read through? Who does something different?

Ask for suggestions about how they could prepare to read, such as previewing the pictures and headings, skimming over the information in the pages, and thinking over what they already know about the topic.

Discuss the strategies of skimming and scanning. **Skimming** is used to get an idea of what a text is about. It involves looking over large sections of text line by line without reading every word. **Scanning** is used to locate a specific keyword or fact. It involves moving the eyes down the centre of the page and stopping to read each time a keyword is reached. Ask students to describe when they have used skimming and scanning. You can let them compare and contrast the two strategies by having them draw a Venn diagram. Students can work with partners or in small groups to fill in the two overlapping circles.

Strategy Spotlight: SQ3R, page 97, can be used to introduce or reinforce the strategy of surveying, questioning, reading, reciting, and reviewing texts. Have students practise using the technique, then ask for feedback on their successes or difficulties with it.

Do It Differently: Here's a practical suggestion to make to students: some readers benefit from being able to mark the text as they read, highlighting interesting or important information and circling points they don't understand to revisit later. Students could also use sticky notes to flag parts to return to after they have an overview of the whole section.

Plug It In: Some readers who struggle with understanding text are good listeners or viewers. Help them make sense of information in other formats, using visually striking CD-ROMs or Web sites. Make use of Web sites with audio components, or record texts ahead of time for students to use.

THREE STEPS FOR FINDING ANSWERS

Objective: *to increase awareness of reading strategies*

Skills at Work: *integrating, summarizing, synthesizing*

Activity: *partner work, discussion, BLM: What's on the Box?*
(p. 117)

Call for each student to bring in a cereal box (or collect over several weeks so they can work together in pairs). Discuss: What kinds of information can you find on the outside of a cereal box? Then direct students to complete BLM: What's on the Box?

When they're finished and have compared their answers, talk about which strategies they used to find the information. Point out the three basic steps they followed: First, they predicted what they would find; second, they read the information; and third, they considered the meaning of the information they found. Bring out the point that readers get much more out of information if they prepare beforehand and think about it afterwards.

Strategy Spotlight: Using Reading Strategies, page 98, can be used to discuss and reinforce reading strategies. You may wish to introduce strategies one at a time, and provide ample time for students to practise using them.

Strategy Spotlight: Reading Strategies Summary, page 99, can serve as a reference or allow students to record information as they read a selection. Alternatively, you might have students work with Strategy Spotlight: Using Reading Strategies to create their own point-form summary of strategies.

Think About It: Invite students to explore these questions in a journal entry: Which reading strategies have you used? Which have been the most useful? Why? What would you like to improve about your reading skills? Why? How could you improve your skills? What would you be able to do with your new skills?

Take It Further: Activities that students could use to practise making sense of information include finding the cost of items in a catalogue or flyer, finding information in a television guide or phone book, choosing a route on a map, solving math problems, and reading instructions to board games or video games. Provide plenty of opportunities for readers to work in pairs and share and discuss what they have read.

MAIN IDEA ANALYSIS

Objective: to identify main ideas

Skills at Work: analysing, deciding, evaluating, integrating, summarizing

Activity: listening, discussion, BLM: What's the Main Idea? (p. 118)

Model reading an informational text for the class. Choose something relatively complex (with paragraphs more than a few sentences long) that connects to a topic under study. You may wish to have students read along with an overhead or handouts, or simply have them listen.

Read the first sentence and the last sentence of the first paragraph, then ask: What do you think is the purpose of this paragraph? What questions do you have about it? Then real aloud the whole paragraph and ask: What is the main idea of the paragraph? Write a summary of students' responses on the board.

Go through paragraph by paragraph like this, then take a look at main ideas on the board and ask: What is the main idea of the whole text?

You may wish to tie this activity in to a lesson on topic sentences, and have students notice how the main idea of each paragraph relates to the topic sentence of that paragraph. Students can practise writing topic sentences for subjects they are interested in. Provide students with a handout of text that is not broken into paragraphs or sections. Instruct them to determine where it should be broken and create a heading (or a summary of the main idea) for each section. They could then use BLM: What's the Main Idea? to analyse the content further. Alternatively, the blackline master could be used to deconstruct another text they are working with.

Take It Further: Find examples of challenging texts that students are currently working with, and have partners work together to rewrite the text in a more simplified way. Remind them not to leave out any information.

Plug It In: Bookmark or list Internet sites and create questions for students to answer when they visit the sites, based on the main idea of each.

ORGANIZATIONAL PATTERNS

Objective: to recognize organizational patterns

Skills at Work: analysing, classifying, deciding, identifying, organizing, synthesizing

Activity: group work, discussion, text exploration

Give groups of students a collection of words, phrases, sentences, and/or pictures about a topic. Ask students to imagine they are writing a report about the topic. Which order will they put the items in? How will they organize them? Each group can share and compare its methods with another group and note similarities and differences. Then groups can report on their methods and a list of different organizational methods can be made on the blackboard.

Discuss with students that understanding written material includes figuring out what kind of organizational pattern is being used. Textual cues show how the information is organized. Certain words and phrases, such as "for example," "most important," "but," "therefore," and "on the other hand," alert the reader to important information. Examples of organizational patterns appear in Strategy Spotlight: Organizational Patterns, page 100. However, to make the patterns more relevant to students, examples should also be found in texts that the students currently work with. The patterns can be introduced over several days, so that students have time to become familiar with each type. Students can use their knowledge of organizational patterns to organize their own writing. Assign students paragraphs to write about current topics, grouping information according to one or more of the patterns. They can work with the same information each day, rewriting it to follow different patterns.

After identifying organizational patterns, students can work with partners or individually to create a reference chart of textual cues (organizational patterns and signal words) to guide them through reading and writing expository text. Dictionaries and thesauruses could be helpful sources of more cues.

Related lessons on categorizing can be found in Chapter 7, Organize and Record Information.

Take It Further: Ask students to locate several biographical texts about a famous person. Which use time sequence to describe the person? Can they locate a biographical text that uses another pattern?

UNDERSTANDING VISUAL INFORMATION

Objective: to identify steps

Skills at Work: analysing, identifying, integrating, synthesizing

Activity: modelling, application

Choose a diagram with many parts or labels. Display it on an overhead projector and suggest to students that although the diagram might seem complicated, by examining it step by step it will become easier to understand. Apply Strategy Spotlight: Understanding Illustrations, page 101, for them. Then students can follow the steps using an illustration from a text they are currently studying.

Take It Further: Have students examine captions accompanying pictures in magazines, newspapers, and other reference sources. What do students suggest is the purpose of a caption? Tell them to note which captions provide more information than is shown in the photo and which merely describe what is there. Students can cover up the captions and create their own, then exchange with other students. They can also consider the pictures they are using in a project and write captions for them.

TAKING STEPS ONE AT A TIME

Objective: *to identify steps of a task*

Skills at Work: *analysing, deciding, identifying, integrating, synthesizing*

Activity: *brainstorming*

Ask students to share experiences they've had following written instructions (such as those with a board game or model toy, or those that came with an assignment). What was easy? What was challenging? What would they do differently next time? With the class, brainstorm suggestions for strategies to use when following directions and record the ideas. Then, compare the class list to Strategy Spotlight: Following Instructions, page 101. Ideally, you would now give them a written set of instructions for a task, such as an assignment or project, and let them put their strategies to use.

Take It Further: To gain practice in both writing and reading directions, partners can write a list of directions for each other for tasks such as building a block structure or drawing certain shapes.

PERSUASIVE FORMATS

Objective: *to recognize persuasive texts*

Skills at Work: *analysing, deciding, evaluating, identifying*

Activity: *class discussion, charting*

Depending on students' background knowledge, you may wish to begin a discussion by asking students to define *persuade*. What are some synonyms? (convince, influence, win over, talk into). Prompt students to describe when they have recently tried to persuade someone of something. Were they successful? What happened? What would they do differently next time?

In persuasive writing, the author tries to get the reader to accept a personal opinion, and the reader's job is to sort the facts from the opinions. Select a piece of persuasive writing, such as a newspaper editorial, to read to the students. Ideally, it could tie in to texts or projects the students are working with. If possible, project the text on an overhead for students to follow. Then ask students these questions: What are the facts? How can you tell? Which words signal bias? How can you tell? Who says so? (or: How many people say so?) You might also go through the text sentence by sentence, asking whether each sentence states a fact or advances an opinion, or both. If students are unsure, have them consider what question the sentence answers. Watch for questions that lead the reader to a particular response.

Direct students to choose a topic they would like to convince someone of. They can list information in two columns: one of the facts, the second of details or reasons that back up each fact. Then they can write their persuasive paragraphs and exchange with partners for feedback on how persuasive they were.

A related lesson on facts and opinions can be found in "Fact versus Opinion" in Chapter 4, Identify and Evaluate Sources, Materials, and Tools.

Take It Further: Have students watch and analyse television commercials, with these questions in mind: Which are aimed at students your age? How can you tell? How would the producers of the commercials describe their audience?

SETTING A PURPOSE

Objective: *to connect purpose and strategy*

Skills at Work: *analysing, deciding, identifying, summarizing, synthesizing*

Activity: *class discussion, group work*

Discuss with the students the importance of setting a purpose before reading a text. How does the purpose affect a reader's interpretation of the text? What are some purposes they might have for reading?

Have students form into several groups. Give each a different purpose for reading the same selection, such as to summarize the selection, to think of questions they'd like to ask the author, and to form and back up opinions about key points. If the text has a variety of photos, illustrations, or charts, have one group summarize and pose questions about the graphics. Another group can analyse the author's use of language and conventions.

Then have students report their findings to the class and discuss again the questions from the beginning of the lesson.

CURRICULAR CONNECTIONS

Objective: *to extend comprehension skills into other subject areas*

Skills at Work: *analysing, identifying, integrating, synthesizing*

Activity: *creative partner work; advice column writing; class discussion and graphic organizer work*

Reading comprehension skills are necessary in other subject areas. You might wish to use the following activities to extend students' skills.

MAKINGS MAPS MAKE SENSE

Invite students to work with partners to create a storyboard for a segment on a TV show about "How to Make Sense of a Map." They might put their instructions into a musical or rhyming format. Tell them that their description should include explaining a legend, compass rose, and scale.

MAKING MATH MAKE SENSE

Encourage students with math difficulties to write to a "Math Columnist" ("I get frustrated doing word problems. What should I do?"). Class members can take turns answering the letters with their suggestions for strategies. You might want to pass out Strategy Spotlight: Making Math Make Sense, page 102, for their reference.

Plug It In: Give students a problem to solve collaboratively using a spreadsheet.

Ask students: What strategies do you use when you watch an informational video, such as a science or nature program? What helps you remember what you learned? Have students mention specific nonfiction videos or programs that they have seen and found inspiring. Why were the videos inspiring? Students' recommendations could be listed to form a reference for the classroom. ("You've got to see this!") They could design a graphic organizer for recording information from a video, then try it out, either in class, or at home watching a science or nature program. Invite them to report back to the class on their results and on refinements they would suggest for the organizer. Students could use Strategy Spotlight: Watching Informational Videos, page 102, as a base for their ideas.

Thinking Strategies

THINKING ABOUT INFORMATION

Objective: *to appreciate thought*

Skills at Work: *generating, integrating, summarizing, synthesizing*

Activity: *discussion, writing/art*

Ask students to respond to these questions: How important is thinking about what you have read? Is it enough to just read something? What does thinking about it add? You may wish to discuss the statement that "a house is more than a collection of bricks" — that something more is added when all the pieces are in place. Ask students to relate the statement to how information is transformed into knowledge through the thinking process. Students could respond to the quotation with a journal entry, by a three-paragraph personal essay, by a poem, a poster or a collage, or in another written or visual format.

Student Self-Assessment

Have students consider their reading comprehension and work habit skills. What are their strengths? What would they like to improve? Students can reflect on these questions, then formulate short-term and long-term goals. Encourage students to keep a written record of their goals handy for reference and refinement.

How can you decide if a book will be a good resource for you to use? Follow these simple steps to evaluate it.

1. What does the publication information tell you?

Look on the first few pages for the name of the publisher and date of publication. Is the book recent? Unless you're researching a historical subject, you'll probably want up-to-date resources. Do you recognize the author's name? Where was the book published?

2. How is the book organized?

Turn to the table of contents. Check if any chapter headings refer to your topic. Then turn to the index at the back of the book. Can you locate many of your keywords? How long is the book? Does it seem to have too much detail?

3. How interesting are the pictures?

Skim through the pages. Do the pictures spur you to find out more? Read some of the captions. Do they supply the sort of information you're after? Are there graphs, tables, or other illustrations to help explain information?

4. How easy is the book to read?

Turn to a section that might be useful to you. Read the first paragraph in the section and the last paragraph. Does it cover the type of information you want? If you're not sure, read the first sentences in each paragraph for an overview. If the text seems too difficult, find an easier source.

A Helpful Hint: Check out these two good sources when you begin your research.

(a) Encyclopedias provide a general overview of topics and can help you think of other keywords and phrases or parts of your topic to research further.
(b) Children's nonfiction books are easy to read and give a broad overview of a topic.

Strategy Spotlight: Electronic Search Tools

1. Are you ready to search?

There are two things you need to know before you begin a Web search:

> You can't search the Web directly — you can only search databases.
> There isn't one search tool that catalogues the whole Web.

What do these statements mean? The first means that you need to know how to use search tools. The second means that you will need to try more than one way to find information.

   Here are a few of the tools at your disposal:

Subject directories — subjects arranged in categories - Web pages are found and added by people. - You search for the category your subject is in. - Examples: **www.yahoo.com**; **www.Brittanica.com**	**Search engines** — search for the keywords you enter - Web pages are found and added by machines. - Sometimes they have directory listings. - Examples: **www.askjeeves.com**; **www.altavista.com**
Metasearch engines — search other search engines and databases - They report about 10 per cent of finds from each search engine visited. - Examples: **www.metacrawler.com**; **www.dogpile.com**	**Subject guides and specialized databases** - These offer collections on a subject, usually compiled by experts. - Some use keywords; some have directories. - Examples: Argus, Clearinghouse, WWW virtual library

2. Which search tools will you use?

If you're after broad, general knowledge, start with a subject directory, subject guide, or database. If you have a specific question you want to answer, start with a search engine or a metasearch engine.

3. What if you don't find what you're looking for?

If you're using a subject directory, try looking in a different category or directory. Is there any other name your subject could be classified as?

   If you're using a search engine, use more than one keyword for your search. Use keywords that are unique to your topic. Try other search engines.

   In both cases, if you find something that seems close, check out the Web page. Maybe it links to something useful.

4. When you find what you're looking for . . .

Evaluate the site and the information. Is it true? Is it useful? Is it recent? Share information about the best search strategies with your classmates.

When you arrive at a Web site there are a few questions you need to answer before you decide whether to use the information published there.

1. Does the Web site suit your topic?

Skim through the contents of the home page, which provides an introduction to what can be found at the site. Check listings in the index. Decide whether the information there will probably be useful, easy to understand, and provide the right amount of detail. If so, go on to question 2. If not, find another site and repeat this step.

2. What type of Web page is it?

If you linked to it from a good site, that's a recommendation. The address can provide an important clue about the type of information at the site:

.org an organization promoting an idea
.com a business promoting a product
.edu an education site, usually presenting factual information
.gov a government site, usually presenting factual information

Who is responsible for the site? Find the author's name (usually at the top or bottom of the page). When was the site posted or last updated? Is it recent? If you're satisfied with the answers to these questions, go on to question 3. If not, find another site and repeat step 1.

3. Is the information accurate?

This question is sometimes tough to answer, but it's very important. You cannot assume information is correct because it's on the Internet. Anyone can publish anything on the Internet. It's up to you, the viewer, to ask yourself, "Does the site contain facts or opinions? How can I make sure the information is accurate? Does the author want to convince me of a certain point of view? Do I agree with the author's viewpoint? What's the purpose of the site — to inform, to entertain, to persuade, or to express? How do I feel as I view the site?" When the author's viewpoint is easy to detect, it is called an **explicit bias**. If it is hidden, it is called an **implicit bias**. Even if the site contains only facts, the author may have used them to express his or her opinion. Be alert!

Strategy Spotlight: Interview Tips and Techniques

Use these tips and techniques the next time you conduct an interview.

A. Getting Ready for the Interview

1. **What is your purpose in doing the interview?**
   What do you want to find out? It is easier to ask good questions if you have background knowledge. Find out all you can about the topic and the person you're planning to interview.
2. **Brainstorm a list of questions, then choose the best ones.**
   Use 5WH questions, or questions that ask for more than a yes/no answer. Try to select questions that only the person can answer. Some questions can ask for facts, and others for opinions. The questions you ask depend on your purpose and topic. Prepare six to eight questions for a 15-minute interview. You may not need to use them all.
3. **Think about the order of your questions.**
   Does it seem logical? Would a different order work better? Decide which questions are most important for your purpose. Ask those questions first.
4. **How will you record the interview?**
   If you want to use a tape recorder, ask your subject for permission, then practise using the machine. If you are taking notes, be prepared to abbreviate words that are likely to come up.
5. **When you contact your subject to schedule the interview, be able to explain your purpose in a sentence or two.**

B. During the Interview

1. **Listen actively.**
   As your subject answers, think of follow-up questions you would like to ask. Jot these down and ask them when appropriate. Don't interrupt your subject in the middle of an answer.
2. **Be ready to change the order of your questions.**
   If you ask one question and your subject talks about something you were going to ask later, switch to the new topic.
3. **Take lots of notes during the interview, even if you are taping it.**
   If you don't understand an answer, ask your subject to explain it a different way. If you need more time to write an answer, politely ask your subject to wait while you finish.
4. **You might make a few notes about how your subject looks and acts.**
   These details could be used later to enrich your writing.
5. **Thank your subject for the interview.**
   Check whether you can contact him or her later if you have further questions.

C. After the Interview

1. **Rewrite your notes.**
   As soon as possible after the interview, review your notes and clearly rewrite words that were scribbled. If you think of new questions, write them down. You might be able to ask your subject these questions later, or you might be able to find the answers yourself.
2. **Choose the direct quotations you would like to feature.**
3. **Choose words carefully.**
   You don't have to use every word your subject said. You can shorten the answers as long as you don't change the meaning.
4. **Consider what ideas you can add to your writing folder to follow up later.**
5. **Evaluate your role in the interview.**
   Did your questions get the information you wanted? Did you listen attentively? How could you have improved the interview? What will you do differently next time you interview someone?

Strategy Spotlight: How to Write a Bibliography

A bibliography is a list of the information resources used. The sources might include books, magazines, encyclopedias, and Web sites. In a bibliography you organize information about the publications, listed alphabetically by the authors' last names.

There are different styles, or types, of bibliographies. One style you can follow is outlined below.

Book

1.   Name of author or authors (period)
     —   last name first (comma) first name(s) — Betty Woods becomes Woods, Betty
     —   If there are two or more authors, only the first author is listed last name first: Woods, Betty, Edward Smith, and Julie Tang.
2.   Year of publication (period)
3.   Title in italics (period)
     —   If you are writing by hand, underline the title; on computer, use italics.
4.   Place of publication (colon)
5.   Publisher (period)

Sattler, Helen Roney. 1995. <u>Our Patchwork Planet</u>. New York: Lothrop, Lee & Shepard Books.

Magazine or Newspaper

1.   Name of author or authors (period) (the same as for books)
2.   Year of publication (period)
3.   Name of the article in quotation marks (period inside marks)
4.   Title of the magazine in italics (comma)
5.   Issue of the magazine in parentheses (colon)
6.   Page numbers of the article (period)

Jacob, Katherine. 2000. "Family Reunion." <u>Equinox</u> (Vol. 18.6 #108): 50.

Encyclopedia

1.   Name of the encyclopedia in italics (period)
2.   Year of publication (period)
3.   Volume number (comma)
4.   Article name in quotation marks (comma inside marks)
5.   Page numbers of the article (period)

<u>World Book Encyclopedia</u>. 1996. Vol. 19, "Turtles," 522–523.

Web Site

1.   Name of author or authors (period) (same as for books)
2.   Date of the document or its last revision (period)
3.   Title of the section or page in quotation marks (period inside marks)
4.   Name of the whole article in italics (period)
     (If #3 and #4 are the same thing, then treat it as #4.)
5.   Site address (URL)
6.   Date you visited site in parentheses (period)

Mayell, Hillary. 1999. "Unraveling the Mystery." <u>Secrets of the Elephant Seal Revealed</u>. www.ngnews.com/news.asp (7 January 2000).

Strategy Spotlight: Can't Find What You Want on the Web?

Have you ever had trouble finding what you want on the Web? Try these solutions to your search problems.

1. Are you using phrases rather than single words for keywords?

If not, do it!

If so, try a variety of combinations of keywords. Try the same keywords on different search engines. Use synonyms.

2. Have you tried several different search tools (search engines and subject directories)?

If not, do it!

If so, rethink your search. Are you getting hundreds or thousands of hits for your request? Be more specific. Are you getting only one or two hits for your request? Check out the sites in case there are interesting links. Then broaden your topic and try again. Check the Help listing for each search tool. Are you entering keywords in the recommended format?

3. Is the address coming back as not found?

Try these solutions:

- Check your spelling. One of the most common problems is making a mistake typing in the address.
- The server might be down or very busy. Try again later.
- Try omitting the filename at the end of the URL.
- The file might have been moved or removed. Don't take up too much time trying to track it down.

4. Consider using another resource.

It can sometimes be difficult to locate what you want on the Web, even if you are doing all the steps correctly. Try using a print or human resource instead.

When you're using print resources, put these handy hints to use:

1. Start with resources that are easy to read and easy to work with.

2. Check the publication date. Use recent resources for most topics.

3. Check the table of contents. Decide if the book is about the subject you want.

4. Check for your topic keywords in the index.

5. Before you read thoroughly, skim and scan the section. Make sure it has the information you need. Read the headings. Look at the pictures.

6. Connect what you read to information you already know.

7. Try to get a variety of viewpoints on issues.

8. Check your facts with more than one source.

9. Make notes in your own words. Write down questions and your reactions to the information you record. Make a note of important sections to come back to and read again later.

10. Record bibliographic information for all your sources.

11. List facts and ideas to follow up.

12. Consider non-print resources as well as print resources. Is there a video or audiotape that might provide information about your topic? Have you searched Web sites or interviewed authorities?

When you want to read information and understand it, try SQ3R!
SQ3R stands for

Survey — Question — Read — Recite — Review

1.   **S:** First, **survey** what you're going to read. Scan over the pages, looking at the headings, glancing at the charts and pictures, and reading the introduction and summary (or opening and closing paragraphs).

   Now you have a general idea of what the information is about. Go on to the "Q."

2.   **Q:** Turn the headings into **questions**. For example, if a heading is "The Water Cycle" turn it into "What is the water cycle?" or "How does the water cycle work?"

   Now you have a more specific idea of what you might find in each section. Go on to the first "R."

3.   **R:** Slowly **read** one section at a time. Watch for key examples and definitions. How does the text answer the question you made? Examine the charts and photographs that accompany the text. How do they connect with what you are reading?

   Now you have more information about the topic. Go on to the second "R."

4.   **R: Recite** or **record** the main points of what you just read. Don't look back at the information, just use what you remember. If you record them on a graphic organizer, you can use them later for notes.

   Now you know the points you remembered from your reading. Go on to the third "R."

5.   **R: Review** what you just read. Reread the introduction and summary and review the section, watching for any main points you missed. Record these points along with your list from the second "R." How does it all fit together? What do you know now that you didn't before?

   Now you're ready to go to the next section or topic and repeat these steps.

Survey — Question — Read — Recite — Review

Reading strategies can help you understand and remember what you read. Ask yourself the following questions. They can help to keep you focused and alert.

Before Reading

1. What do I already know about this topic?
Make a web or list of information you already know. Think about stories, poems, magazines, videos, CD-ROMs, or Web sites you have discovered that relate to this topic. Share your knowledge with a partner and listen to what your partner knows.

2. Why am I reading this?
Think of questions you have about the topic. Decide what you would like to find out. Talk about your ideas with a partner.

3. How is the text organized?
Read the title and think about what clues it gives you. Skim over the text and read the main headings and any words in boldface or special fonts. Look at the pictures and read the captions. Note where there are charts, lists, or bullets. If you notice new or difficult words, jot them down and find out what they mean before you read. There might be a glossary or definitions included in the text.

During Reading

4. What happens next?
Jot down questions as you read. Watch for answers in the text. Predict what you'll find in the next section. Keep asking questions and predicting answers.

5. What does it mean?
Reread a sentence that you don't understand. Then read all the sentences around it. If it doesn't make sense, mark it, take a guess, and read on. There might be more information later in the section that will explain it.

6. How does it connect?
Imagine how your topic looks or sounds. Imagine yourself as part of the topic. Think about how it connects to something you already know.

After Reading

7. What did I learn?
Make jot notes of what you learned. Compare your list with a partner's. Retell all you can remember to a partner. Identify the most important idea. Identify the most interesting idea. Represent the information in a sketch, cartoon, poem, or chart.

8. What did I miss?
Reread the text. Check unfamiliar words with a partner or in a dictionary. Be alert for details you might not have noticed the first time through.

9. What does it mean?
Connect the information to yourself, to other texts, and to the world. Decide how this information fits in with other information you know and why it is important. Consider how you can use the information. Think of questions about the topic and ways you can find out more.

This summary will remind you of reading strategies you can use. You might choose to make a check mark next to a strategy each time you use it. What other strategies can you try?

Before Reading

1. Think about what you already know.
2. Establish a purpose for reading.
3. Skim over the text.

Other strategies I can use:

During Reading

1. Ask questions.
2. Predict what comes next.
3. Picture the content.
4. Read on.
5. Connect the content to something you know.

Other strategies I can use:

After Reading

1. Share what you found out.
2. Read again.
3. Determine the main idea.
4. Connect the idea to something else you know.

Other strategies I can use:

Some common ways of ordering information, as well as related signal words and phrases, are listed on this page. What other signal words and phrases do you know for each pattern? Add them to the lists. Study the pattern examples provided below. Find or create your own examples and add them in the appropriate places.

Sequence

Events are put into an order according to when they happened.
Words to watch for: until, before, after, next, first, on (date), at (time)

Example: First, mix together the flour and water. Next, add the sugar. Stir until it has dissolved.

Question and answer

The author asks, or refers to, a question, then suggests possible answers.
Words to watch for: who, what, where, why, which, how, the question is, the answer is, it could be that, maybe, one may conclude

Example: The question is "How many farms will be affected?" The answer may be surprising.

Problem and solution

A problem is stated and one or more solutions are considered.
Words to watch for: one reason, a solution, a problem

Example: It can be difficult to teach a puppy to obey. Taking the puppy to obedience school is one solution.

Cause and effect

Something is shown to be the cause of certain effects; an effect is traced back to its cause(s).
Words to watch for: since, because, on account of, due to, then, so, therefore

Example: The unusually wet spring is being blamed for the record number of mosquitoes.

Comparison and contrast

Two or more things are compared and the similarities and differences are shown.
Words to watch for: similarly, however, the difference between, but, as opposed to, after all, however, yet, nevertheless

Example: The eastern chipmunk eats insects, slugs, and worms, but the yellow pine chipmunk eats mainly seeds.

Even the most complex diagram can make sense if you follow a few simple steps.

1. Start with the whole.

What questions do you have when you look at the illustration? What would you like to find out about it? List your questions.

2. Move on to the parts.

Start on one part of the illustration and move around in an order. Read captions or labels as you go.

3. Think about how the parts are connected to the whole.

How do the parts work together? What categories could you make for the parts?

4. What have you learned?

Which of your questions were answered? Which questions do you have now? Explain what you know to a partner.

Strategy Spotlight: Following Instructions

If you are baking a cake, assembling a toy, or doing a science project, it helps to follow instructions. Use the three steps outlined below.

1. Start with the whole.

Scan the list of instructions to determine what you are going to be doing. Don't try to understand them the first time through, just look over the whole list to get a sense of what is going on. Think of questions as you scan.

2. Look at the parts.

Go back to the beginning and read the instruction one at a time. Watch for keywords, such as active verbs, that give you direct instructions. Underline the keywords and picture yourself doing the action.

3. Think about the whole.

Have all your questions been answered? Is there any part you do not understand? What do these instructions enable you to do? How does that ability fit in with other information that you know?

Think About It: How does knowing how to follow instructions help you to create good instructions? How can you use these skills outside of the classroom? Answer these questions with a journal entry.

Strategy Spotlight: Making Math Make Sense

If solving math problems is a problem, try these strategies. Exercise patience and be willing to go step by step.

1. Start with the whole.

Read the whole problem through once. What is it asking?

2. Break the problem into parts.

What information is in each part? Which pieces of information will help solve the problem?

3. Look at it a different way.

Draw a picture or make a chart or graph. Think about similar problems you have solved before. What helped you to figure them out?

4. Take a guess.

Try an answer that might work. What does it tell you about the real answer?

Strategy Spotlight: Watching Informational Videos

What strategies do you use when you watch an informational video or documentary? What new strategies could you try from the list below?

1. Establish a purpose for viewing.

What do you already know about the topic? What do you wonder about the topic? What do you hope to learn from the video? Make a note of your questions.

2. Be an active viewer.

Think while you watch. Predict what will happen next. Ask questions. Pay attention to sounds as well as sights. Jot down ideas.

3. Consider what you have learned.

Which of your questions were answered? Which new questions do you have? What interesting ideas would you like to follow up? Use a few sentences to summarize the content to a partner.

Primary and Secondary Source Checklist

It's important to understand the nature of your research sources and to ensure that you have a balance. Make a check mark to show whether each resource is primary or secondary. Then add five more resources to the list. Trade with a partner, and check off each other's resources as primary or secondary.

	Primary	Secondary
an audiotape of a speech		
copies of letters		
encyclopedia		
TV news coverage		
TV news commentary		
field research		
diary		
a personal essay		
a magazine article about famous explorers		
an artifact in a museum		
an interview reprinted in a magazine		
a textbook		
1.		
2.		
3.		
4.		
5.		

Classroom Resources

Consider which resources in your classroom might contain information about your topic.

1. My topic is, as follows (identify your topic in the form of a question):

2. Keywords for my topic:

3. People in the classroom who could help me:

4. Encyclopedias I could check (include the volume numbers):

5. Books in the classroom I could use:

6. Magazines in the classroom I could check:

7. CD-ROMs I could use:

8. Vertical files I could use:

9. Databases or directories I could use:

10. Other resources in the classroom I could use:

Library Checklist

Do you know where the resources listed below are located in your library? Check off each as you find it and provide a concrete example. Explain when you would use it in the far right column.

Resource	Example	When would you use this resource?
❏ periodicals (newspapers and magazines)		
❏ vertical files (collections of articles)		
❏ books in other languages		
❏ encyclopedias		
❏ dictionaries		
❏ catalogue (card or electronic)		
❏ computer terminal(s)		
❏ librarian's desk		
❏ audiotapes		
❏ videotapes		
❏ CD-ROMs		
❏ fiction		
❏ nonfiction		
❏ new books		

Library Scavenger Hunt

A good way to become familiar with the physical layout of the library is to go on an information hunt. Search for these resources in the reference section or nonfiction stacks of your library. Use the library catalogue to help you in your search.

A. Write the name and call number of an example for each.

   1. a rhyming dictionary _____

   2. a book about art history _____

   3. a cookbook _____

   4. a collection of folk tales _____

   5. a book about deserts_____

   6. a book of world records in sports_____

   7. a book about bicycle repair _____

   8. a biography_____

   9. a book on how to speak a foreign language _____

   10. a book about computer graphics_____

B. Look in the stacks and find a book you would like to read in each of the following sections. Write down the name and call number of each. Then choose one of the books and check it out to read!

   390 (between 390 and 400) _____

   560 (between 560 and 570) _____

   630 (between 630 and 640) _____

   910 (between 910 and 920)_____

Fact and Opinion

Do you know the difference between fact and opinion? A fact is something known to be true; an opinion is a view or judgment. For each topic given below, write one fact and one opinion.

1. Topic: Weather

   Fact:

   Opinion:

2. Topic: Advertising

   Fact:

   Opinion:

3. Topic: The Internet

   Fact:

   Opinion:

4. Topic: Rock Concerts

   Fact:

   Opinion:

5. Topic: Space Travel

   Fact:

   Opinion:

6. Topic: Orange Juice

   Fact:

   Opinion:

7. Topic: Movies

   Fact:

   Opinion:

8. Your own choice of topic:

   Fact:

   Opinion:

Think About It

How will you use your skill in determining facts and opinions? Name several occasions where it will be useful.

Compare and Contrast Technologies

What works better? Why? Compare and contrast each pair by listing the advantages and disadvantages. Is one clearly better than the other? What conclusions do you draw? Write your conclusions in the space provided. For no. 3 create your own comparison of two different technologies used to do similar things.

	Advantages	Disadvantages
1. (a) television		
(b) making your own entertainment		

Conclusion:

2. (a) computer word processing		
(b) handwriting		

Conclusion:

3. (a)		
(b)		

Conclusion:

Think About It

Read over your conclusions. Are speed and convenience always best? Explain your answer.

Web Site Evaluation Form

Use this form to help you evaluate a Web site. For each question give the site a score from 1 (poor) to 5 (excellent).

Site Name: _____   Date Visited: _____

Site Address: _____

Content
How useful was the content?

____ /5

Accuracy
Did the information seem reliable (from a recognized source)? Was the site updated recently?

____ /5

Presentation
How interesting and inviting was the site?

____ /5

Ease of Navigation
How easy was it to move around the site?

____ /5

Your Comments

The best thing about this site was

_____

Think About It

What would you change to improve this site?

Web Users, Beware!

Here are a few signs that tell you to beware of the information published on a Web site. How many of these warning signs have you noticed on Web sites? Check off any you've seen.

Check with a parent or teacher before using a site that

___ asks for money or a credit card number

___ asks for your home address, phone number, or other personal information

___ has many spelling, grammar, or punctuation errors

___ has threats, is trying to scare you or make you feel guilty

___ tells you to pass information to other people

___ seems to be only opinions and emotion

___ makes claims but doesn't back them up with facts

___ doesn't tell who the author is or how to contact the author

___ tries to persuade you by giving only one side of the issue

What other warning signs have you noticed?

Think About It

How will knowing these signs help you find good information on the Web?

The Search

Fill in this form to help you keep track of information sources you are using to complete your project.

My Topic:
(phrased as question)

What I Found Out

People I spoke with

_____   _____
_____   _____
_____   _____

Places I visited

_____   _____
_____   _____
_____   _____

Books I used

_____   _____
_____   _____
_____   _____

Web sites I visited

_____   _____
_____   _____
_____   _____

Other sources I used

_____   _____
_____   _____
_____   _____

What I still want to know

_____   _____

Resource Checklist

Which resources have you used for your project? Place a check mark next to each source you consulted. Write the name of the resource in the space provided. Consider using some of the other resources on this list for your project. Your teacher might want you to hand in this form with your completed project.

❏ almanacs _____

❏ atlases _____

❏ audiotapes _____

❏ CD-ROMs _____

❏ classmates _____

❏ community elders _____

❏ databases _____

❏ dictionaries _____

❏ electronic networks _____

❏ encyclopedias _____

❏ experts _____

❏ family members _____

❏ friends _____

❏ librarian _____

❏ library catalogue _____

❏ magazines _____

❏ museums _____

❏ newspapers _____

❏ nonfiction books _____

❏ public library _____

❏ reference books _____

❏ school library _____

❏ teacher _____

❏ telephone books _____

❏ thesauruses _____

❏ videotapes _____

❏ Web sites _____

Other resources I used:

Change the Questions

Each of these interview questions is asking for a yes/no answer. Reword each question so that it is asking for more complete information.

1. Is this interesting work?

2. Do you like your job?

3. Was it hard to get hired?

4. Are some things easy about this job?

5. Are some things hard about this job?

6. Did you get your skills at university?

7. Did you have good teachers?

8. Would you encourage students to consider this profession?

9. Do many people have the skills for this job?

10. Do you have anything else to say?

Think About It

Read over your questions. Why are they better than the original questions? How can you use this skill in your daily life?

Survey Plan

Use this page to plan your survey.

1. Why are you conducting a survey? (What is your purpose? What do you want to find out? What do you predict the results will be?)

2. How will you collect information? (oral or written survey? target group — what type, how many, how participants selected?)

3. What type(s) of questions will you use? (multiple choice? ranking? open-ended?)

4. What do you plan to do with the results? (write a summary, make a graph, present to class) How will you connect your results to your prediction? Use this space or another page to list the questions you plan to ask. Make your questions as specific as possible.

Recording Resources

Use this form to keep track of the resources you use.

1. Book

   Author:

   Year of publication:

   Title:

   Place of publication:

   Publisher:

   Page(s):

2. Magazine or Newspaper

   Author:

   Year of publication:

   Name of article:

   Title of magazine or newspaper:

   Issue (month or day):

   Page(s):

3. Encyclopedia

   Name of the encyclopedia:

   Year of publication:

   Volume #:

   Name of article:

   Page(s):

4. Web Site

   Web site address (URL):

   Author:

   Date of the document:

   Title of the section or page:

   Date you visited site:

5. CD-ROM

   Title:

   Year produced (if shown):

   Name of section or article:

Encyclopedias

Encyclopedias offer comprehensive information on particular branches of knowledge, usually in alphabetically arranged articles.

Do you know your way around one? Test yourself with these activities.

1. Name a sport or hobby you are interested in.

2. Look up your topic in the index (usually the last volume of the encyclopedia). Record all the listings for volumes and page numbers:

3. Find the first listing. Turn to the article. What are the guide words at the top of the page?

4. Look at the pictures or charts (if any). Read the captions. If there is something that you didn't know about your topic, write it here:

5. Find three points you didn't know about your topic in the article and write them here in your own words:

6. At the end of an encyclopedia entry there are often cross-references that tell you about other articles on similar topics. List any cross-references your article provides:

7. If you still wanted more information after reading this article, name two steps you could take:

What's on the Box?

What kinds of information can you find on a cereal box? You'll find out as you answer these questions!

A. Before you read, answer this question:

   What information do you think you will find on the cereal box?

B. Find the information and write it in the blanks:

   Name of cereal

   Name and address of the company

   Ingredients

   Serving size

   Servings per package

   Calories per serving   without milk   with milk

   Does this cereal contain sugar? If so, how much per serving?

   Which vitamins and minerals are in the cereal?

   Which additional vitamins or minerals are added with milk?

C. Think about what you found out.

   What other information is on the box?

   If you were designing this cereal box, what would you change to make it more appealing to someone your age?

   What would you change to make it more appealing to an adult?

What's the Main Idea?

If you want to make sense of information, figure out the main idea. Complete these points for each paragraph of challenging reading.

1. Topic sentence:

2. My own one-sentence summary of the paragraph:

3. Keywords in this paragraph:

4. The most important idea in the paragraph:

5. I know this idea is important because

6. Words I don't understand:

7. Questions that I have:

Part C

The Transformation of
Information

Organizing and Recording

Model note taking for students. Take notes while watching a video, then share them with students using an overhead projector. Point out your use of abbreviations, phrases rather than sentences, paraphrasing, and ways you indicate ideas to follow up or questions you have. Invite students to share the strategies they use to take notes and to identify the areas in which they would like to improve their note-taking skills.

Hand out photocopies of an information selection that students can mark up. As a class, read through it paragraph by paragraph. After each paragraph decide what, if any, information needs to be recorded in note form. Ask students to paraphrase it briefly, then share their versions. Some students might find it easier to highlight important information first, then paraphrase it. Point out how much information was condensed into just a few words, and that it was not necessary to copy out entire sentences. To consolidate understanding, distribute and discuss Strategy Spotlight: How to Take and Make Notes, page 130.

Take It Further: Students could take turns being the Note Taker of the Day. The note taker would take notes while the class watches videos or listens to selections read aloud. The notes could be copied each day and distributed to other students. Let everyone take a turn.

Discuss these questions with students. You may wish to record and tabulate responses on the board.

- How can you use the word-processing features of a computer to help you organize and record information? (use style, font, cut and paste; import and incorporate graphs, charts, data, spreadsheet into text; convert digital files by opening and saving them as different file types)
- How does a spreadsheet help? (use sum, product, quotient, and average)
- How can a group use a computer to collect, store, retrieve, and organize their data? What are the advantages and disadvantages to using a shared folder?

Extend this lesson by having students work in groups to design, create, and modify a database for a group project that you would like them to complete.

Plug It In: Have students visit a museum, science, or art gallery site and create an advertisement for it by organizing and rearranging information downloaded from site. Students can copy, import, or download pictures or sound files to create a multimedia presentation.

CAPTURING THE ESSENCE

Objective: *to use summary skills*

Skills at Work: *analysing, identifying, integrating, organizing, summarizing, synthesizing*

Activity: *note taking, making summaries*

Have students take notes about a guest speaker, a video or other presentation, or a selection that is read aloud. Then students could write a summary from their notes, retelling in their own words all the important parts and accurately portraying the information given. Let students exchange summaries or read them aloud so that the content and retelling can be compared.

To offer students some guidance on summarizing, distribute and discuss Strategy Spotlight: Making a Summary, page 131. Students could build on that by creating a brochure or press release based on a longer article, such as an encyclopedia entry as source. Limit them to a certain number of words to fit onto the brochure (perhaps a quarter of the original number, depending on students' abilities), and remind them to include all the important information in a logical order and write the summary in their own words.

Take It Further: Have students write a one-paragraph summary about their topics. They can then use each of the sentences to start a new paragraph, and so create a report on their topic.

THE VALUE OF CATEGORIZING

Objective: *to recognize categories*

Skills at Work: *classifying, identifying*

Activity: *game playing, BLM: Category Connections (p. 142)*

Categorizing is the first step in creating an outline. Ask students for their explanations and examples of categories (divisions based on a similar characteristic). Point out categories in the classroom to get them started. Some examples are resource books, writing implements, and storage compartments.

Students could play a word game with partners. Each partner can make a list of words and the other can figure out what category they have in common. Students may be able to identify more than one category for each group of words. Then they can complete BLM: Category Connections, individually or with partners. If students are working on a project, tell them to read over their notes and select categories that the notes could belong to.

Take It Further: How are categories helpful in daily life? Ask students to imagine a supermarket, department store, or bookstore without sections. What would the experience of shopping be like?

What would their favorite movie be like if the scenes were presented in a different order? Students can represent their responses with a cartoon, comic strip, humorous poem, or flow chart.

USING CATEGORIES IN OUTLINES

Objective: *to create and use outlines*

Skills at Work: *analysing, classifying, deciding, identifying, integrating, organizing*

Activity: *discussion, sorting*

Ask students to imagine what a book would be like if information was written without any order. Read students a short paragraph with the words or sentences in a scrambled order. Can they make sense of it? Order helps the listener or reader to absorb information.

An **outline** is a way of creating order in notes. It identifies the main categories, then groups the supporting key points in their proper categories. Give students an example by writing the following list on the board: oranges, pineapples, tomatoes, avocadoes, potatoes, and carrots. What categories can students suggest for these words? (perhaps Fruits, Vegetables, and Uncertain, or Food That Grows Above the Ground/Below the Ground, or Edible/Non-edible Peels, and so on). Write the categories on the board and then have students guide you in listing the items under each, as shown below.

I.   Food That Grows Above the Ground
    A. oranges
    B. pineapples
    C. tomatoes
    D. avocadoes
II. Food That Grows Below the Ground
    A. carrots
    B. potatoes

Point out that the names of the categories become headings and are numbered. The supporting key ideas are lettered and indented. (Note: In a formal outline, major headings have Roman numerals, then capital letters, then numbers, then lowercase letters. If students are unfamiliar with Roman numerals you might wish to introduce them, or simply use numbers for headings and lowercase letters for supporting key points.)

Invite students to think of another way to show the categories (such as a web with rays for each main idea and the other information grouped around). Distribute Strategy Spotlight: Graphic Organizers, page 35, and ask students to identify which strategies they have used and which they might use next. Then they can choose a method for outlining a current research project.

Do It Differently: Let students make an outline, as in the example above, then cut it apart line by line and exchange with a partner to put it back in order again. If the partner chooses a different order than the original one, they can discuss the advantages of each.

Some students might find it easier to work with pictures at first. Present them with three basic backgrounds to represent headings, then let them work with sorting or drawing pictures (representing details) onto the correct background.

Plug It In: Let interested students investigate any computer task wizards that are available for outlining information and share their discoveries with the class. If students have entered their notes into a computer, they can shift the most important items to the top of the page and format them to use as headings. Then the remaining points could be arranged under the headings using cut and paste. This strategy could be the beginning of a rough outline.

Take It Further: Have students locate and read an informative and interesting article from a magazine or Web site (you could prepare a list of sites in advance for them to use). Ask them to summarize the article in a few sentences, create an outline for the article, and list three questions that the article did not answer. Tell students to hand in a copy of the article along with their work.

Student Self-Assessment

How do students rate their skills in making connections, organizing, note-making, and summarizing? How could they improve these skills? Have students formulate goals in these areas and determine measures of their success. Students can refer to these goals over the coming weeks and refine them further.

Chapter 8

Evaluate Information to Gain New Understanding

Evaluate Information

If students haven't yet made a web of all the information they have found for a project, have them do so now. They can highlight important information with one color, and mark information they found interesting with another color. Students can then summarize the information in different formats, such as a story, an opinion, or a lesson. Their summaries can include how the information connects to themselves, to their family or community, and to the world.

You might want students to complete BLM: Evaluate Information to evaluate their project information.

Think About It: Invite students to explore these questions with a journal entry: What new understanding do I have as a result of doing this project? How can I use the information I've learned from the project outside of school? How can I use the skills I've gained from the project in other situations?

Take It Further: Ask students to create a list of main points about their topic that could help someone else who wishes to study it. These summary points could be collected into an anthology and added to each year to become a classroom resource.

This activity can be done using project information or a current community issue. If using a community issue, supply information in the form of newspaper or magazine columns, letters, or articles. Ask students to identify the issue, decide how they feel about it, then look at evidence of other points of view. If there is not adequate information about other points of view, encourage the students to imagine them. Consider the reasons and facts that support the various sides. Invite students to consider if and how their initial bias has changed as a result. Then ask them to complete BLM: Forming Opinions.

Objective: *to identify needed information*

Skills at Work: *analysing, deciding, generating, identifying, integrating, speculating*

Activity: *creation of word problems*

Invite students to consider the amount and type of information needed to solve a problem. They can create written problems for each other to solve that contain too much information, too little information, or just the right amount of information. Partners can identify which information is needed, add any missing pieces, and solve the problem. The topic of the problems can connect to other subjects being studied, such as math problems about the current unit or social studies problems about maps, statistics, or global issues. Students might also suggest recipes or instructions that have too much or too little information.

Plug It In: Students can pose problems for one another and test solutions using computer-assisted design (see Glossary) to create a model. In each instance they can assess whether more information is required.

EVALUATION OF VISUALS

Objective: *to analyse visual formats*

Skills at Work: *analysing, evaluating*

Activity: *small group work, making lists*

What makes a good photo for a nonfiction text? What qualities does a good illustration have? Direct students to work in small groups to examine a number of photos and illustrations in nonfiction texts and develop a list of criteria for each. Their analyses might include line, form, color, texture, shape, balance, and composition; overall impression; the mood, emotion, or theme conveyed; and the measure of how realistic or unrealistic each is. They can choose examples of the best and worst in each category, then present their findings to the class. Tell them to include an analysis of the captions that accompany the visuals. Students could also cover up the captions and experiment with language to create effective new ones that include interesting details.

To guide students in their analysis, they might consider how the colors, subject, and style make them feel, how a visual is similar to or different from other artwork they've seen, what the artist's purpose might have been, and whether that purpose is fulfilled.

Take It Further: Suggest that students make a photo essay or collage about their topic, applying what they have learned. Tell them to include captions.

Draft Information

THE NATURE OF DRAFTING

Objective: *to develop a draft*

Skills at Work: *organizing, synthesizing*

Activity: *class discussion, writing*

Ask students to share what they know about the process of writing a rough draft. Make sure that they understand that the draft does not have to be perfect and that they shouldn't worry about spelling (ask why not). Distribute Strategy Spotlight: Drafting, page 132, and discuss the points together. Then students can prepare a rough draft of their project.

Objective: to evaluate research by considering the steps

Skills at Work: identifying, integrating, summarizing, synthesizing

Activity: flow chart making, BLM: Reflecting on the Research Process (p. 145)

Evaluate Research Process

Ask students to make a flow chart of steps they have followed with research projects from inception to drafting. Next to each step they can record why the step was important, what was accomplished, and what they might try the next time they follow the process. They should include the following steps which can be represented in a variety of orders with arrows indicating lots of movement: selecting a topic, purpose, audience, and format; summarizing prior knowledge, brainstorming; formulating questions; creating a plan; identifying and evaluating sources, materials, and tools; accessing information; making sense of information; recording and organizing information; and evaluating information to gain new understanding. (Students might identify the steps by other names.) They can then complete BLM: Reflecting on the Research Process.

Student Self-Assessment

Ask students to consider their skills in evaluating information, thinking critically, and creating drafts. What areas for improvement are they aware of? What steps can they take to make improvements? Have students record their goals for future reference and refinement.

Chapter 9

Share What You Know

Giving and Receiving Feedback

TAKING THE DRAFT FURTHER

Objective: *to evaluate a draft*

Skills at Work: *analysing, deciding, evaluating, identifying*

Activity: *discussion, BLM: Taking the Draft Further (p. 146)*

Discuss this question with students: Should you start revising your draft as soon as you've written it, or should you let some time pass first? Time allows a writer some distance to better evaluate the writing. When students return to the draft, they should be looking for what is good as well as what needs improvement. Ask students to consider: When you ask someone for feedback on something you've written, what do you want to know? (ideas on how to improve what you've done, what is working well and what is not, and how to change your writing so that it is clear and strong, without obstacles for your reader) List their responses on the board. The discussion could continue with these questions: When have you especially appreciated getting feedback? Describe a time when it was useful. Have you had experience getting feedback that wasn't useful? How did you feel? How did you respond?

You could conclude the lesson by distributing and discussing Strategy Spotlight: Giving and Receiving Feedback, page 133, and BLM: Taking the Draft Further.

Revising

RE-VISION

Objective: *to revise the draft*

Skills at Work: *deciding, evaluating, integrating, organizing, problem solving, synthesizing*

Activity: *discussion*

Print the word "revision" on the board. Ask the students to examine the roots and describe the meaning (re-vision: to see again). How does "seeing again" explain the process of evaluating and revising a draft? Offer students Strategy Spotlight: Revising, page 134, to help them evaluate and improve their drafts. If they are working on computer, encourage them to save and label all drafts. Remind them to double- or triple-space their drafts. Discuss the points together. Suggest that students work with the feedback they've received and follow the steps of the Strategy Spotlight.

LEADS, ENDINGS, AND TITLES

Objective: *to write strong leads and endings*

Skills at Work: *analysing, deciding, evaluating*

Activity: *finding models, charting, writing*

While students are revising their drafts, they can work with leads and endings. Have them work individually or with partners to analyse good leads and endings from magazine stories and categorize the various types. They can consider: What is there about the lead that captures the reader's attention and makes us want to read more? Are there techniques that professional writers use that we can make use of? What might they be?

Create a class chart of various types of leads students identify, such as leads in the form of a question (Did you know that some lizards run on water?), hints at what is going to happen (When I started following the lizard I had no idea of its remarkable ability), leads that speak directly to the reader (You may not know one of nature's oddest creatures), and leads that tell surprising information (Something incredible happens when a basilisk meets water). Have students create three or four different types of leads for their writing and then choose what works best.

A similar process can be followed to identify strong endings. Some common techniques include restating the main idea, connecting back to the lead, raising a question for the reader to consider, and summarizing the most important points.

As with the above activities, students can follow a similar process to identify titles that catch their interest and apply the same techniques to their writing.

Take It Further: With the class's input, create a list of favorite leads from nonfiction material.

THE SOUND AND SUBSTANCE OF LANGUAGE

Objective: *to improve structure*

Skills at Work: *analysing, identifying*

Activity: *reading aloud*

At each stage of the revision process it is helpful to read the piece aloud to hear the flow of words and ideas. Have students read their pieces aloud, checking for the sound of language — do some sentences feel too long or too short? Are there some words that don't sound right and need to be replaced? Is the type of language used (formal or informal) appropriate for the audience and purpose? Students may find it helpful to work with Strategy Spotlights: Sentence and Paragraph Structure, Proofreader's Marks, and Proofreader's Checklist, pages 135–37, to revise their drafts.

FINISHING TOUCHES

Objective: *to polish presentation*

Skills at Work: *analysing, celebrating, deciding, identifying, synthesizing*

Activity: *discussion, review*

Polishing

Depending on the formats students will be using, distribute and discuss any or all of Strategy Spotlights: Oral Presentations, Visual Presentations, Writing to Inform, and Offering and Defending an Opinion, pages 138–41. You may wish to provide students with a style sheet for written projects they will be submitting. Double spacing is a common requirement. Consider whether they will need to follow header, footer, and margin specifications. Will they provide a table of contents, bibliography, or index? Tell students to assess whether they have polished the presentation so it presents no obstacle to the listener, reader, or viewer. Students can take a look at the whole research process as they complete BLM: Research Process Checklist (p. 147).

Plug It In: Specify and discuss the type and style of font for the project, depending on the audience. Serif fonts are easier on the eye, larger type is easier for young children to read, and so on.

Take It Further: Students could structure a mini-lesson for the class to teach what they have learned.

Student Self-Assessment

In which ways could students improve their abilities to work a draft into a polished publication? Students could reflect on this question in a journal entry, then formulate a list of specific goals and a timeline for meeting them.

Strategy Spotlight: How to Take and Make Notes

Note taking helps you to break information into smaller, more manageable parts. Note making helps to keep you alert and processing information while you read, listen, or view.

Two-Column Notes

Two-column notes are a simple way to organize and record your notes. Divide a page in half and name each column. Use the headings that follow or make your own names for the columns.

ALTERNATIVES:

1. Call the first column **Note Taking**. Record facts and quotations.
    Call the second column **Note Making**. Write your responses, questions, and ideas about each of the facts and quotations that appear in column one.

2. Call the first column **Main Ideas** and the second column **Details**.

3. Call the first column **Interesting Facts** and the second column **Important Facts**.

4. Call the first column **Opinions** and the second column **Proof**.

More Tips

* If you're not using columns, leave a wide margin on one side of your notes to identify the topics. These notations will help you locate information when you come back later to review.

* Divide a page into four sections. Give each the name of a heading from the selection you are taking notes from. As you read, record the main ideas and important facts under each heading. Use as many pages as you need for headings.

* Use short phrases, not complete sentences. Use abbreviations and symbols.

* Use your own words. Don't copy unless you want to include a quotation that you will credit to the source. If you use a quotation, make sure you copy it exactly.

Strategy Spotlight: Making a Summary

Taking notes breaks a large piece of information into parts. Making a summary puts the parts into a new "whole." These are some steps you can follow to make a summary:

1. **Read over your notes and think about what you have learned about the subject.**
    Use your prior knowledge to help understand and evaluate new information. How does this new information fit in with what you already know?

2. **Use 5WH questions to help you identify the most important information.**
    Have you answered all those questions in your notes? (Who, What, Where, When, Why, and How)

3. **Think about the order you will put information in.**
    Consider using an organizational pattern, such as cause and effect, problem and solution, question and answer, description, sequence, or compare and contrast.

4. **Use the questions below as a checklist for the rough draft of your summary.**

    *   Is the summary brief?

    *   Is it accurate?

    *   Is it in your own words?

    *   Does it include the most important information and ideas?

    *   Does it include supporting key points?

    *   Is there anything missing?

    *   Does the order make sense?

    *   Does it show the author's point of view and ideas?

    *   Does it include your reaction to the information?

Strategy Spotlight: Drafting

Are you a writer or a critic? Both roles are part of the writing process, but not at the same time. When you're creating a draft, remind the critic in you to take a break. Drafting is not a final step. A draft gives you something to work with and refine. Remind yourself of the following points when you are writing a first draft:

1. Once you begin writing, try to keep going without stopping. Time yourself for 15–20 minutes. The purpose of this time is simply for getting your thoughts onto paper. You're producing a rough draft — something that's not expected to be perfect. If you catch yourself trying to reword a sentence to make it sound right, remember that revision comes later. Just get your thoughts down in whatever form you think of. If you have two ways of saying something, put them both down.

2. Give yourself lots of space. Double-space if you are using a computer. Double- or triple-space if you are handwriting. Later, you'll use the space for making changes or additions. Use only one side of the paper so you can cut and rearrange pieces in the revision stage.

3. If you can't think of how to say something, or spell something, you can just draw a line or make a question mark and keep going. Don't stop now to track down the information, use the spell check, or count the number of words. You can do those operations later.

4. You don't have to write in order. Start with whatever section you wish, and if you get stuck, move on to another section. Later you can cut and paste parts into the correct order.

 © 2000 *Information Transformation* by Tricia Armstrong. Permission to copy for classroom use. Pembroke Publishers.

What is an easy and effective way to improve your writing? Ask for feedback! Share your writing with someone you trust.

A. Asking for Feedback

1. Ask for feedback from someone who has the skills and knowledge to help you improve your writing. Introduce your writing by describing what your purpose is, who your audience is, and what you want to learn from the feedback. Point out specific areas or questions that you want feedback on.

2. Note what your partner thinks is good about the piece as well as what needs more work.

3. Accept suggestions for improvement. Make a note of the suggestions and consider whether they would work for your piece. Ask someone else for feedback if you have any doubt.

4. Ask for elaboration on any point you are not sure of. Thank the person for the feedback.

B. Giving Feedback

1. Ask the writer what he or she would like feedback on. Listen carefully to the response. Read the whole piece before giving suggestions.

2. Point out what is good about the draft. Comment on which elements work especially well and what impression you get.

3. Phrase your ideas as suggestions, not as criticisms. Be specific in what is needed. For example: "This part could use a little more explanation" is more constructive than "This is not good."

4. Ask whether the writer wants more detail.

Revising your work means to "see it again." One strategy of "seeing it again" is to hear it. Read the draft aloud to consider the flow and order of ideas. Are any parts missing? Don't worry at this stage whether every word is exactly right. Look at the overall organization of your work. When you've identified changes you want to make, work in the order of these steps:

1. Cut.

Is there any unnecessary information?

Are some paragraphs too long?

Do I repeat myself?

Does each section serve my purpose?

2. Rearrange.

Is it easy to pick out the main idea of each paragraph?

Would the information work better in a different order?

3. Add.

Are there any loose ends?

Did I answer all the questions my audience might have?

Do some parts need more detail and explanation?

4. Rewrite.

Did I use friendly language that shows my enthusiasm for the subject?

Are there any words or ideas I should explain better?

As you read your work aloud, ask yourself, "Are all my sentences complete sentences? Does each sentence include a subject (person or thing doing the action) and a verb (action word)?" Think about these questions as you read:

1. Types of sentences

Should any of the shorter sentences be combined?

Should any of the longer sentences be broken into several sentences?

Are there some longer descriptive sentences?

Are there some shorter sentences?

Is there an occasional question or exclamation to add impact?

2. Paragraph structure

Does each paragraph have a topic sentence?

Do all the other sentences in the paragraph tell about the topic sentence?

Is the topic sentence interesting?

Do all the sentences in the paragraph belong?

Are the sentences in a good order?

You can devise your own set of symbols for proofreading, or you can use the same symbols that professionals do. Some key proofreading marks are outlined below. Find each of the symbols used in the sentence that follows.

insert, add this ∧

delete ℓ

period ⊙

comma ∧

capital letter ≡

lower case /

start a new paragraph ¶

insert space #∧

close up ⊃⊂

transpose ∿

¶ after you have made your main major revisions, you are ready to proof read for your work punctuation, grammar and Spelling⊙

Strategy Spotlight: Proofreader's Checklist

After you have made your major revisions, you are ready to proofread your work for punctuation, grammar, and spelling. Go slowly, word by word, as you proofread so you can catch any errors or notice if words are missing. Remember, you are reading what you have written, not what you think you have written!

Use this checklist to guide you through the proofreading process.

Punctuation

1. Does each sentence start with a capital letter?
2. Does each sentence have end punctuation?
3. Have I capitalized words correctly?
4. Do my contractions have apostrophes?
5. Have I asked a partner about punctuation I'm not sure of?

Grammar

1. Does each sentence complete a thought?
2. Do the subjects and verbs agree (singular/plural)?
3. Do verb tenses agree?
4. Are my pronoun references correct (e.g., two brothers/they)?
5. Have I asked a partner about grammar I'm not sure of?

Spelling

1. Does the spelling of all words look right and feel right?
2. Have I checked words that are easy to confuse?
3. Have I checked words that I've misspelled before?
4. Have I used a dictionary or computer spell check?
5. Have I asked a partner about spelling I'm not sure of?

Style

1. Do my headings and subheads look consistent?
2. Have I presented any drawings or tables in a consistent way?

If your teacher has provided you with a style sheet, check that you have followed the instructions.

Strategy Spotlight: Oral Presentations

Preparation and practice can help to make an oral presentation smooth and easy.

Feedback is an important part of preparing an oral presentation. Practise in front of a mirror, ask a partner for feedback, or use an audio- or videotape to record your presentation. Focus on skills you want to improve. Think about your reasons for sharing your information with an audience. Practise your presentation several times before real or imaginary audiences. Imagine yourself giving a smooth and polished presentation. And remember: If you're interested in what you have to say, your audience will be too.

The following points can help you prepare your presentation:

1. **Think about the effect you want to create.** Experiment with using these techniques, then choose what works best for you:

    (a) **Volume**: Make sure you speak loudly enough for all members of the audience to hear you. If you are not sure, ask whether the people at the back of the room can hear you. Consider emphasizing certain key words by using a slightly louder voice.

    (b) **Speed**: Be careful not to speak too fast. Slow down or pause for important words, phrases, or headings.

    (c) **Pronunciation**: Practise speaking clearly and carefully. Try not to slur words or leave off endings. Remember that your real audience may be hearing your points for the first time and won't know what you're saying if the words aren't clear.

    (d) **Expression**: How you express emotion in your voice can emphasize key points and create interest. Consider using different pitches — a higher or lower — for certain sections. And don't underestimate the value of dramatic pauses.

2. **Body language is an important part of an oral presentation.** Be sure to make eye contact with various members of the audience. Use gestures when appropriate, and try not to fidget or sway.

3. **You might wish to summarize your presentation on note cards.** Try to prepare well enough that you don't need to read the presentation word for word. Put some of your information in visual aids or props, such as posters, flip charts, or overhead projections. If you are using electronic equipment, check it in advance to make sure it's working properly and you know how to use it.

Be an active viewer. Look at posters, billboards, photographs, and drawings. What attracts your attention? Use some of the same techniques in your own visual presentations. Keep these points in mind as you create:

1. Purpose

What is your purpose in making a visual representation? Do you want to persuade, express, inform, or entertain? Is the message or the image more important? Or are they both equally important? How can you use your words and images to convey your purpose?

2. Audience

Who are you trying to reach with your message? What are they likely to notice and respond to? What do you want your viewers to think and feel when they see your message? Will people have to come close to get your message, as with a photo collage, or can they stand far back, as with a poster or mural?

3. Format

Which format will you use? If you want to attract people from a distance, consider using bright colors and few words. If you want to create a mood, think about how the color scheme, lettering, and layout work together. Try different fonts or design your own lettering, but make the words easy to read. Put the most important information in larger letters, and the details in smaller letters.

Experiment with the layout by putting the text and pictures in different places. Make several drafts or "mock-ups" and choose the best elements of each.

Take plenty of time for the planning stage. If you are using electronic equipment to present your work, check it in advance to make sure it's working properly and you know how to use it.

When you are writing to inform, think about your audience. You have information about a subject that you are sharing. Make it easy for your audience to see why it is interesting and important to gain the new knowledge. Use these points to guide you in your writing:

1. Decide what is important.

Start by taking a look at the information you have collected. Summarize your most important information in a few points. Turn each of the points into a question that your reader might ask. Make a list of information you want to be sure to include. Check over your list. Are there any main points that are missing? Are there any points on the list that don't need to be included?

2. Put the information in order.

Consider the beginning and the end of your selection. Catch the reader's interest by using an exciting or interesting lead. Within the first few sentences, clearly show the reader what the topic is and why it is worth reading about. Also consider what you want the reader to see last. Sometimes, important information is emphasized if it appears at the end of a selection. You can organize the body of the selection using any of these ordering techniques that suit your information:

- by importance (most important to least important, or the other way around)
- by difficulty (easiest to most difficult to understand)
- by position (describe the topic from left to right, foreground to background)
- from general to specific, from main ideas to details

3. Make the information easy to understand.

Information is easier to understand if it includes illustrations or examples. Consider adding drawings, charts, photographs or diagrams. Include comparisons or anecdotes, if appropriate. Consider arranging your text to include bulleted or numbered points, or use a question-and-answer format.

4. Take the role of the reader.

As you read your draft aloud, imagine yourself in the role of your reader. What questions would you ask? Which parts might be difficult to understand? Is the information complete, logical, and accurate? Do the main ideas stand out clearly?

Strategy Spotlight: Offering and Defending an Opinion

Do you have an opinion you want to share? Do you have a solution to a problem, or a point of view about an issue? Is your view worth defending? If so, consider using any of these formats: letter to the editor, review, report, speech, advertisement, business letter, advice column, or opinion article. Keep the following points in mind as you organize your ideas.

1. Imagine that your audience has not yet formed an opinion on the issue.

Consider that your job is to explain your information so clearly, accurately, and completely that your audience will see the validity of your point of view.

2. Be clear about the subject and your opinion.

Show why the issue is important for the audience. Then take a firm stand and state your opinion simply and clearly.

3. Support your opinion with facts and examples.

Use details to make the facts come alive for your audience. Include anecdotes, personal experiences, and observations if appropriate. Can you find statistics or quotations from experts to back up your viewpoint? Be sure to state the sources of all your facts. The use of good sources will add strength to your arguments. Double-check all your facts and figures. Your audience should be able to trust your information.

4. Acknowledge other viewpoints.

People have different opinions. It is in your favor to recognize other opinions and explain how your arguments and information are stronger or more convincing. Be aware of the strengths of other viewpoints and consider dealing with them one by one. Assume that your audience is informed, reasonable, and interested in these viewpoints.

5. Close strongly.

Use your concluding remarks to summarize your point of view. Suggest what action your audience might take. You might wish to end with a question.

Category Connections

A. Name five different ways of categorizing each group.

Television programs

Students in your school

Food that you eat

Countries of the world

Music

B. Name three ways categories are used in each of these subjects.

Science

Social Studies

English Language Arts

Mathematics

Your favorite sport or hobby

Think About It

Create your own categorizing question/activity and exchange it for a partner's. Do the partner's question.

Evaluate Information

Use these questions to evaluate the information you gathered through your research.

1. What was the main question I was asking in my research?

2. What is the answer?

3. What did I learn that surprised me?

4. Where did I find my best information?

5. Which of my original questions am I still wondering about?

6. Which new questions do I have?

7. Where could I try looking for answers?

Think About It

Why is evaluating a useful skill outside of the classroom? Name several occasions when you could use evaluating skills.

Forming Opinions

What's your opinion? Take a look at it while you answer these questions.

1. (a) What was your opinion before you started your research?

   (b) What evidence did you have to support it?

2. (a) What is your opinion now?

   (b) What new evidence did you find to support it?

3. What personal conclusion can you draw based on the evidence you've found?

4. (a) What other opinions exist about this topic/issue?

   (b) What evidence might support those opinions?

5. Choose a different point of view and create a one-paragraph summary of your information from that point of view. Use the back of this page.

Reflecting on the Research Process

Consider the steps you followed when researching. To gain some perspective on your work, answer the sentence stems below.

1. The easiest step was

    because

2. The most challenging step was

    because

3. The step that took the most time was

    because

4. I changed my plan in these ways:

5. Some things I would do differently next time. For example:

6. I could have accomplished my goal by making more use of technology in these ways:

Think About It

Why is it important to review and adjust your plan while you research?

Taking the Draft Further

Will you be developing your draft further? Would you like to take it through the steps of revision and proofreading and then publish it? If so, use these questions to help you assess your draft.

1. How could this draft better suit my purpose?

2. How could this draft better suit my audience?

3. What is my choice of format for this draft? Why?

4. How could I improve my graphics and captions?

5. What are the best parts of my draft? Why?

Here is what I plan to do next:

Research Process Checklist

In order to complete a research project effectively, you need a variety of skills. Use this checklist to review the steps of the research process. Check steps you know how to do. Circle the skills you would like to improve.

The Research Plan	The Search for Information	The Transformation of Information
I can	**I can**	**I can**
_____ choose a topic	_____ identify tools, materials, and sources of information	_____ record observations
_____ identify my audience		_____ organize information in a variety of ways
_____ establish a purpose	_____ evaluate tools, materials, and sources of information	_____ assess my format choice
_____ consider possible formats		_____ record information (make notes)
_____ use my knowledge and experiences	_____ access print information	_____ evaluate the information I've collected
_____ review my previous knowledge	_____ access human resources	_____ form an opinion
_____ ask questions	_____ access electronic information	_____ write a draft
_____ create a plan	_____ conduct field research	_____ revise, edit, and polish a written presentation
	_____ gather data	_____ revise, edit, and polish an oral presentation
	_____ make sense of information	_____ revise, edit, and polish a visual presentation

Appendix 1
How Can You Show What You Know?

ABC book	character sketch	directions	historical fiction
acknowledgment	chart	directory	history
acrostic	charter	discussion	horoscope
activity book	checklist	display	how-to
adaptation	choral reading	draft	illustration
advertisement	choreography	drama	instructions
advice column	cinquain	drawing	intercom message
agenda	classification	edict	interview
album	classification chart	editorial	invention
analogy	cloze	electronic folder	invitation
analysis	cluster	e-mail	jingle
anecdote	collage	emblem	job description
announcement	collection	epic	joke
answer	column	epitaph	joke book
application	comic strip	essay	journal
art	commentary	eulogy	label
article	commercial	evaluation	leaflet
artifact	compare/contrast	exam	learning log
audiotape	comparison	exhibition	legend
audition	composition	experiment	lesson
autobiography	conclusion	e-zine article	letter
award	concrete poem	fable	letter to the editor
ballad	conference	fact	limerick
banner	confession	fact file	list
bibliography	constitution	fairy tale	log
billboard	contract	feature	logo
biography	construction	feedback	lyrics
blueprint	conversation	field guide	magazine
board game	costume	film	magazine article
book	couplet	flip book	manifesto
book jacket	court trial	flow chart	manual
book report	critique	folder	map
book review	crossword puzzle	folk dance	mask
booklet	curriculum vitae	folk tale	memo
brainstorm	dance	forecast	memoir
broadsheet	database	form	memorial
brochure	debate	formula	mentor
bulletin board	decision	free verse	menu
bumper sticker	definition	friendly letter	mime
business letter	demonstration	game	mind map
caption	depiction	game board	mini-centre
card	description	glossary	minutes
card game	design	goal	mobile
cartoon	diagram	graph	model
catalogue	dialogue	graphics	monologue
category	diamante	greeting card	mosaic
CD-ROM	diary	group discussion	multi-media
certificate	dictionary	haiku	mural
chant	digest	handbook	music
chapter	diorama	headline	myth

narrative poem
native dance
news
newspaper
newspaper article
newspaper ad
notes
notice
novel
nursery rhyme
obituary
observation
ode
opinion
oral report
organizer
outline
overview
painting
pamphlet
panel discussion
papier-mâché
paragraph
paraphrase
parody
pastiche
pattern
petition
photo essay
photographs
picture
picture book
placard
plan
play
poem
policy
poll
portfolio
portrait
postcard
poster
prayer
précis
prediction
press release
proclamation
profile
project cube
proposal
prospectus
prototype
proverb
publishing
puppet play

puzzle
quatrain
question
questionnaire
quiz
radio play
radio show
rap
rebus story
recipe
reference
regulation
report
report card
representation
reproduction
research report
response journal
resumé
review
riddles
role play
routine
rubrics
rule
schedule
scene
science fiction
scrapbook
script
scroll
sculpture
self-assessment
self-help
seminar
sequence chart
sermon
shape poem
sign
simulation
sketch
skit
slide show
slogan
sociogram
solution
song
sonnet
speech
spreadsheet
stage play
stamp
statement
story
storyboard

strategy
summary
survey
syllabus
symbol
synopsis
synthesis
T chart
T-shirt
table
table of contents
tableau
tape recording
tall tale
tally
tanka
teach-a-class
teach-a-friend
telegram
television program
test
testimonial
testimony
textbook
theory
timeline
tips
tongue twister
transcript
travelogue
tree diagram
Venn diagram
video
want ad
web
Web page
will
word search
worksheet

Other ways:

Appendix 2
Dewey Decimal Classification System

000 Generalities
010 Bibliographies and catalogues
020 Library science
030 Encyclopedias
040 Unassigned
050 General periodicals and indexes
060 Organizations, societies, etc.
070 Journalism
080 General collections
090 Manuscripts and rare books
100 Philosophy and Psychology
110 Metaphysics
120 Epistemology, causation, and humankind
130 Paranormal psychology
140 Philosophical doctrines
150 Psychology
160 Logic
170 Ethics
180 Ancient, medieval, and Oriental philosophy
190 Modern Western philosophy
200 Religion
210 Natural theology
220 The Bible
230–280 Christian theology and practice
290 Other religions
300 Social Sciences
310 Statistics
320 Political science
330 Economics
340 Law
350 Public administration
360 Social services
370 Education
380 Commerce
390 Customs
400 Languages
410 Linguistics
420 English
430 Germanic languages
440 French
450 Italian
460 Spanish and Portuguese
470 Latin
480 Greek
490 Other languages
500 Science
510 Mathematics
520 Astronomy
530 Physics
540 Chemistry
550 Earth science
560 Paleontology
570 Life sciences
580 Botany
590 Zoology
600 Technology
610 Medicine
620 Engineering
630 Agriculture
640 Home economics
650 Business
660 Chemical technology
670 Manufacturing
680 Manufacturing for specific purposes
690 Building and construction
700 Fine Arts and Recreation
710 Civic and landscape art
720 Architecture
730 Sculpture and plastic arts
740 Drawing and decorative arts
750 Painting
760 Graphic arts
770 Photography
780 Music
790 Recreation and performing arts
800 Literature
810 American and Canadian literature
820 English literature
830 German literature
840 French literature
850 Italian literature
860 Spanish and Portuguese literature
870 Latin literature
880 Greek literature
890 Literature of other languages
900 Geography, Biography, and History
910 Geography and travel
920 Biographies
930 Ancient history
940 History of Europe
950 History of Asia
960 History of Africa
970 History of North America
980 History of South America
990 History of other areas

Glossary

Note: Communications technology is an evolving field. New skills, processes, materials, and tools are constantly being created. Existing technology is changing, adapting, and being replaced. For these reasons, a glossary is soon outdated. Alert students to the changing meanings of these words, and suggest they use these definitions as starting points. They could work together to update terms and add new ones that they learn.

Algorithm A sequence of steps, such as in a formula or program's instructions, used for solving a problem

Analog A continuous variable signal or physical system, usually electronically based. Analog devices are used to monitor such activities as temperature (e.g., thermometer) and sound (e.g., telephone). Although some computers are analog, such as those processing varying signals like voltage or frequencies, most are digital. *Contrast with Digital.*

Asynchronous/Synchronous communication Asynchronous means not happening at the same time (e.g., e-mail). Synchronous communication allows participants to send and receive information at the same time (e.g., a "real-time" electronic chat or instant messaging).

Binary, Bits, and Bytes A **binary** numbering system consists of two possible states, such as 0 or 1, on or off, high or low. In digital computers, all input is converted into binary numbers made of 0s and 1s (bits). A **bit** is the smallest unit of information a computer can process. Bits are stored in cells in the computer's memory, in groups called bytes. One **byte** is made of 8 bits and holds one alphanumeric character, such as a letter or symbol.

1 kilobyte (K) holds more than 1000 characters, about one double-spaced page of text.
1 megabyte (MB) is about 1000 times greater than a K.
1 gigabyte (GB) is about 1000 times greater than an MB.
A terabyte (TB) is about 1000 times greater than a GB.

See also Digital.

Bookmark, Favorite A computer feature that lets the user store addresses of favorite Web sites

Boolean A two-valued number system developed by English mathematician George Boole in the mid-nineteenth century (1= true, 0=false). A Boolean search uses "and," "or," and "not" to link search words, allowing for a much more specific search.

CAD (Computer Assisted Design) Software and input devices used to design products, such as in architectural, electrical, and mechanical design. The elements of the graphic object can be isolated and individually manipulated. Similar to a drawing program, but more precise in dimensioning and positioning.

Camcorder A small consumer video camera using VHS or 8 mm tape

CD-ROM (Computer Disc Read-Only Memory) A compact disc format used to hold computer data or compressed audio or video data. It can hold more than 600 MB of data. This type of compact disc can only play back information and cannot record or save material. While an audio CD player cannot play a CD-ROM, a CD-ROM player can usually play audio CDs.

Chat A text-based "real-time" communication between two or more users via computer. Messages are instantly displayed on the screens of other users in the "chat room." *Contrast with Instant Messaging (IM).*

Communications technology Tools, techniques, and processes used to create, store, transmit, receive, organize, and analyze data

Computer A machine that processes information according to a set of instructions

CPU (Central Processing Unit) The main chip in a computer, made of silicon and other materials, and comprising millions of interconnected on/off switches. It communicates with input, output, and storage devices to manage the flow of information.

Copy A function of an operating system used to duplicate information

Cursor A symbol that indicates the contact point between the user and the data displayed on the screen. Cursor keys or a mouse may be used to move the cursor.

Cut and Paste The process of moving a block of text or graphics from one location to another in a document, or from one document to another

Cyberspace A term loosely used to describe communities on the Internet and the on-line world. Used by novelist William Gibson to describe a futuristic computer network

Data In its broadest sense, any form of information, such as files, databases, documents, and video. In a more specific sense, it refers to facts and figures that are processed into information. The singular form is datum.

Data processing The storing, retrieving, and manipulating of data

Database A set of interrelated files that can be accessed, manipulated, stored, and retrieved. An electronic database is managed by a **DBMS (Data Base Management System)** that can find, store, analyze, and print data. Within a database, a **table** is a collection of information about a specific topic, such as a class list. A **field** is a specific category, such as all students scoring above 70 percent. A **record** is one person, place, or thing within a table, such as a student's name.

DTP (Desktop Publishing) The process of creating camera-ready output for commercial printing

Digital The type of signal which is represented by a set of discrete numerical values, such as "0, 1" or "on, off." All common computers are digital. **Digital cameras** record images in digital form by converting the intensities of light into numbers. **Digital communications** includes any system that uses digital signals to send or receive information. **Digital information** includes communications in a computer-readable form. *Contrast with Analog.*

Directory An index of files organized in a hierarchy

Disc/Disk/Diskette A storage device used to store data in a digital form. A diskette, or **floppy disk**, is a flexible disk in a plastic case. A **laser disc** is used to store large amounts of digital information, such as digital video data. Video discs and compact discs are often spelled with a "c"; computer disks are often spelled with a "k."

Discussion group/News group On-line discussion forums on specific topics where users can exchange ideas and information

Document A file created with a word processor

Download The process of copying or receiving data from another computer

Drag To move an object from one point of the screen to another, keeping the object visible throughout the process

Drive *(n)* an electromechanical device that a computer uses to store information. There are a variety of drives, such as hard drive, floppy drive, CD-ROM drive, and DVD drive. *(v)* to provide power and signals

DVD (Digital Versatile Disc, Digital Video Disc) A two-sided optical disc that holds about 28 times the information of the same size of CD-ROM. **DVD-Video** is the movie format, **DVD-RAM** is a re-writable format, **DVD-Audio** plays music, etc., and **DVD-ROM** is like a large CD-ROM.

Electronic bulletin board An electronic message centre for posting and receiving messages

E-mail (Electronic mail) The transmission of memos, letters, messages, files, or multimedia documents over a network. An e-mail address includes the user name and the Internet address of the computer on which the user reads his or her electronic mail. *See also URL.*

Ergonomics The study of physical and mental factors that affect people-machine relationships in work settings in order to limit strain on posture, vision, and so on

FAQ (Frequently Asked Questions) A list of frequently asked questions found with many Web sites, mailing lists, news groups, and products

Fax The transmitting of a coded image of a page between remote locations, using the telephone system

File A collection of data (bytes) stored with an assigned file name

Firewall A software or hardware boundary used to protect information stored in a computer from unauthorized access

Flow chart A graphic representation of the steps or sequence of operations in an information system or program, or in solving a problem

Font A set of characters in a particular typeface design, size, and style

Format *(n)* a pre-established layout for data *(v)* to prepare a disk for use by a certain platform

Grammar checker A software feature that checks the use of grammar in a text

Graphics Information portrayed pictorially, such as illustrations, drawings, or photographs

Hardware The computer (or any physical part of it) and related machinery and equipment

Home page The first page shown when a particular Web site is accessed, or the page that is a browser's starting point on the WWW. In the latter context, any page on the Web can be chosen as the home page.

Hypertext Text that contains **hyperlinks**, highlighted or underlined words or phrases on Web pages that link to other documents or sites with related subject matter. The language used to create WWW documents is called **HTML (Hypertext Mark-up Language)**. HTML codes are used to show how a page is formatted, and to indicate hyperlinks and their URLs. Programs called **HTML editors** (such as Microsoft's FrontPAge) make it possible to create Web pages without learning HTML.

Icon A symbol used on the computer screen to represent a function, process, or object

Import To bring data or information from one format into the format currently in use

Information technology The processes, tools, and techniques used to access, manage, and communicate information

Input To enter data into the computer

Instant Messaging (IM) Similar to chat, except the participants have the choice of whether to allow or invite other participants to join. *Contrast with Chat.*

Internet The world's largest computer network

Intranet A private network of sites and resources only available to members

LAN (Local Area Network) A computer network in a small geographic area, such as a school. *Contrast with WAN.*

Login, Logon/Logout, Logoff To login (or logon) is to enter or gain access to a computer system; logout (or logoff) is to end a computer session.

Mail merge A computer function that allows database information to be merged into word-processing documents, such as in the creation of personalized letters from a mailing list

Media Material that stores or transmits data or information. **Mass media** pertains to communication that has a large public audience, such as television. **Multimedia** involves using two or more mediums in an integrated way, such as combining graphics and sound.

Memory The amount of memory determines the number and size of programs a computer can run at once, the amount of data that can be processed immediately, and the speed at which the programs will operate. **RAM (Random Accessed Memory)** temporarily stores information in a computer. It is lost when the computer is turned off.

Menu An on-screen list of options or software functions

Mind mapping A graphic organizer in which ideas and information are grouped around a topic; also called webbing, clustering, or spider maps

Modem (Modulator-Demodulator) A device that changes a computer's digital signals into telephone audio frequencies, dials and transmits information over telephone lines or other delivery systems, and converts audio frequencies back into digital signals upon reception

Navigate To move or determine position, such as moving to different locations on a Web site

Netiquette Commonly agreed-upon rules of behavior for network users, especially in reference to the Internet

Network A collection of computers and supporting hardware and software that are connected to allow the sharing of data, information, and resources

On-line/Off-line On-line means currently connected to a network, such as the Internet; off-line means not currently connected.

Operating system The software that has the instructions to manage the CPU, peripheral devices, and the processes, memory, and communications of the computer

Peripheral devices Hardware devices connected to a computer, such as a monitor, keyboard, mouse, printer, or scanner

Platform The type of computer (such as iMAC) or operating system (such as Windows 2000)

Presentation software Software for creating multimedia presentations, such as slide shows; usually includes drawing and pointing tools, stock graphical elements, predefined backgrounds and page layouts, sound, and video

Printer A peripheral device that produces a paper copy of computer documents. The higher the resolution, the sharper and more detailed the images produced.

Public domain A product, such as software, text, or graphics, which is not copyrighted and may be freely used or copied

Query A request for information or for a report from a database

Save To copy information onto a storage medium

Scanner A peripheral device that converts text, graphics, or bar codes into digital data

Search engine A program that searches for sites on the Internet or information within a site, based on keywords or phrases

Software A set of electronic instructions that performs a particular task. **Operating software** (such as Windows 2000) controls programs, and **applications software** (such as MS Word) processes data.

Sound card (Sound board, Audio card) An expansion device that plays sound from the computer's sound files through speakers or an external amplifier. Most such devices include **MIDI (Musical Instrument Digital Interface)** capability, which allows music to be played, recorded, and edited through the exchange of data between computers and musical instruments.

Spell checker A software feature that checks the spelling of words in a document. A word that is correctly spelled, but wrongly used is not detected.

Spreadsheet A software calculating tool with a matrix of rows, columns, and **cells** (intersections of rows and columns); can be scrolled vertically or horizontally. The contents of cells, or groups of cells, can be added, subtracted, multiplied, or divided.

Storage device A device, such as a drive, used to place information on a storage medium where it can be kept and later retrieved

Storyboard A scene-by-scene panel or board of rough sketches showing the sequence of events in a multimedia presentation, such as a movie, music video, or television commercial

Telecommunication Communication over a distance, such as telephones and computer networks; can include transmitting and receiving text, data, graphics, video, and sound

Text The words on a computer screen or printed page; can also refer to the format of information, as in "oral, print, and electronic texts"

Upload The transfer of data from the user's system to a remote system

URL (Uniform Resource Locator) A Web address specifying the protocol, host name, and optionally, the port, directory, and file name. *See also E-mail.*

Venn diagram A graphic organizer used to compare and contrast, utilizing two or three overlapping circles

Virus, Worm Destructive software programs that can bring down a computer system; viruses are attached to runable programs and are coded to attach copies of themselves to other programs in the operating system; worms replicate themselves through the disk and memory.

WAN (Wide Area Network) A computer network that spans a wide geographical area, such as a city or country. *Contrast with LAN.*

Window A scrollable on-screen viewing area, usually rectangular, that displays part or all of a file

WWW (World Wide Web, the Web) An Internet service that links a collection of sites comprising hypertext documents, which can include text, graphics, sound, and video, as well as hyperlinks

Recommended Resources

ELECTRONIC RESOURCES

Web sites change and addresses may disappear. Good luck! Below is a sampling of sites that, at the time of publication, provide technology background and definitions:

arapaho.nsuok.edu/~dreveskr/WT.html-ssi
http://www.2learn.ca
http://www.yourdictionary.com
http://techweb.com/encyclopedia/home
http://www.whatis.com
http://www.matisse.net/files/glossary.html

STUDENT RESOURCES

The Maran Graphics staff at IDG Books Worldwide offer a selection of basic computer books aimed at the visual learner. Titles include *Computers Simplified* (1995), *Creating Web Pages Simplified* (1997), *Internet and World Wide Web Simplified* (1995), *The 3-D Visual Dictionary of Computing* (1995), and *Multimedia Simplified* (1995).

TEACHER RESOURCES

Atwell, Nancie. 1998. *In the Middle: New Understandings about Writing, Reading, and Literacy* (2nd ed.). Portsmouth, NH: Boynton/Cook.

Bellanca, James, and Robin Fogarty. 1993. *Catch Them Thinking: A Handbook of Classroom Strategies*. Palatine, IL: IRI/Skylight.

Carroll, Jim, and Rick Broadhead. 1999. *The Canadian Internet Handbook 2000: Lightbulbs to Yottabits*. North York, ON: Stoddart. (this, or a more recent edition)

Cecil, Nancy Lee. 1995. *The Art of Inquiry: Questioning Strategies for K–6 Classrooms*. Winnipeg, MB: Peguis.

Crotchett, Kevin. 1997. *A Teacher's Project Guide to the Internet*. Portsmouth, NH: Heinemann. (this, or a more recent edition)

Foster, Graham. 1996. *Student Self-Assessment: A Powerful Process for Helping Students Revise Their Writing*. Markham, ON: Pembroke.

Freeman, Marcia. 1997. *Listen to This: Developing an Ear for Expository*. Gainesville, FL: Maupin House.

Gardner, Howard. 1999. *Intelligence Reframed: Multiple Intelligences for the 21st Century*. Scarborough, ON: HarperCollins.

Graves, Donald. 1994. *A Fresh Look at Writing*. Portsmouth, NH: Heinemann.

Harvey, Stephanie. 1998. *Nonfiction Matters: Reading, Writing, and Research in Grades 3–8*. York, ME: Stenhouse Publishers.

Moline, Steve. 1995. *I See What You Mean: Children at Work with Visual Information K–8*. York, ME: Stenhouse Publishers.

Morgan, Norah, and Juliana Saxton. 1994. *Asking Better Questions: Models, Techniques, and Classroom Activities for Engaging Students in Learning*. Markham, ON: Pembroke.

Wilhem, Jeffrey D., and Paul Friedemann, with Julie Erickson. 1998. *Hyperlearning: Where Projects, Inquiry, and Technology Meet*. York, ME: Stenhouse Publishers.

Williams, Bard. 1999. *Internet for Teachers* (3rd ed.). FosterCity, CA: IDG Books. (this, or a more recent edition)

Skills Index

(Based on Skills at Work, listed for each lesson plan)

Reproducible Student Page Index

("SS" signifies "Strategy Spotlight"; "BLM" signifies student activity page.)

Part C: The Transformation of Information